r-02

Kentucky

Kentucky

R. Conrad Stein

Children's Press®
A Division of Grolier Publishing
New York London Hong Kong Sydney
Danbury, Connecticut

Frontispiece: A rural Kentucky stream
Front cover: A Kentucky horse farm
Back cover: Louisville's waterfront along the Ohio River

Consultant: Karen McDaniel, Director, Blazer Library, Kentucky State University, Frankfort, Kentucky

Please note: All statistics are as up-to-date as possible at the time of publication.

Visit Children's Press on the Internet at http://publishing.grolier.com

Book production by Editorial Directions, Inc.

Library of Congress Cataloging-in-Publication Data

Stein, R. Conrad.
    Kentucky / by R. Conrad Stein.
    144 p. 24 cm. — (America the beautiful. Second series)
    Includes bibliographical references (p.) and index.
    Summary : Describes the geography, plants, animals, history, economy, language, religions, culture, sports, art, and people of the Bluegrass State.
    ISBN 0-516-20687-7
    Kentucky—Juvenile literature. [1. Kentucky.] I. Title. II. Series.
F451.3.S74 1999
976.9—dc21
                                                              98-14582
                                                                    CIP
                                                                    AC

Acknowledgments

The author wishes to thank the Kentucky Department of Travel in Frankfort for their friendly and helpful assistance in providing materials for this book.

At Churchill Downs

Thoroughbred horses

A long hunter

Kentucky cardinal

Contents

Deer

**Cumberland Gap
National Historical
Park**

Scenic Kentucky falls

Monk Estill

CHAPTER ONE

My Old Kentucky Home

t is said that in 1852 the songwriter Stephen Foster visited his cousin who lived near Bardstown, Kentucky. Foster was so swept away by the beauty of the land and the warmth of his cousin's house that he wrote "My Old Kentucky Home," one of the most moving of his many songs. The house that inspired Foster's song still stands. It is now the centerpiece of a 290-acre (117-ha) nature reserve called My Old Kentucky Home State Park.

Of course this story might be fiction. Historians point out that there is not a scrap of evidence to prove that Stephen Foster ever saw the Bardstown house. Nevertheless, the song stirs the hearts of Kentuckians. In 1928, the legislature chose "My Old Kentucky Home" as the official state song. Though Kentuckians have heard the song a thousand times, they are known to weep at the words and the melody.

Kentucky commands the loyalties of its residents. Citizens regard the state almost as they do their families. Like one's family, the state is a place to love without qualification in times of riches or poverty and during periods of sickness or health.

Kentucky offers its people charms that offset a sometimes sluggish economy. The state's beauty is dazzling. It is called the

Stephen Foster

Opposite: The house that inspired Stephen Foster's "My Old Kentucky Home"

Geopolitical map of Kentucky

Bluegrass State after the delicate blue haze produced by its grasslands in the springtime. Those grasses have long nourished sleek and graceful Thoroughbred horses that race with the speed of the wind. Kentucky also boasts forested mountains, rushing rivers, and Mammoth Cave—the world's longest cave system.

Few residents leave Kentucky out of choice. However, the state's economy, though improving in recent years, has driven many citizens to seek work in more prosperous places. Today, manufacturing is Kentucky's most important industry. In the past, most Kentuckians worked on farms or in coal mines. Prices for coal and farm goods suffer frustrating ups and downs. Rather than cope with the high and low spells, thousands of Kentuckians left their homes to find work elsewhere.

Still, the love of one's home state is the theme of the Kentucky story. Drive the Kentucky highways and you will see license plates from every state in the land. They are not all tourists. Many are

transplanted Kentuckians who moved away to earn a better living for their families. Always they return, if only for a visit. Kentuckians are compelled to come back because no matter where else they live, the Bluegrass State remains home in their hearts.

Kentucky is known for many things, including its Thoroughbred horses.

CHAPTER TWO

"Land of Tomorrow"

The name *Kentucky* comes from a Wyandot Indian word, *Kah-ten-tah-teh*, that has several interpretations. One meaning is "Land of Tomorrow." Still other interpretations are "Meadowland" and "Dark and Bloody Ground." Interestingly, all three variations of the Indian word can be applied to the early history of the state. Kentucky was looked upon as a rich and fertile land by Native Americans and European settlers alike. It was also a bloody battleground where hundreds met their deaths.

Paleo-Indians preparing a mastodon for eating

The First Kentuckians

Some 16,000 years ago, people called Paleo-Indians came from the north and settled throughout the United States, including the Kentucky region. The Paleo-Indians were the first Kentuckians. They arrived while Ice Age glaciers still covered much of North America. The Paleo-Indians used spears to hunt mastodons, mammoths, and other creatures that were once common in the area.

Traces of ancient cultures—gravesites, bits of pottery, and tools—have been found in all of Kentucky's 120 counties. People of the Archaic period (8000 to 1000 B.C.) gathered along riverbanks where they lived on fish and clams. Archaic period men and women apparently valued dogs, because these animals were often buried with them in their graves. Agriculture began during the Woodland

Opposite: The Kentucky River

**Big Bone Lick State Park,
Where the Mastodons Roamed**

Imagine Kentucky as it looked 20,000 years ago. Picture elephantlike mastodons with long, curving tusks and mammoths as big as houses.

Herds of these ancient giants were attracted to a warm spring that still bubbles from the grounds at Big Bone Lick State Park near Covington. Dozens of the beasts became trapped in the marshes, and their fossilized remains can be seen by visitors who come to the park today. ■

period (1000 B.C. to A.D. 900), as people learned to grow squash and gourds. A large Woodland village thrived near present-day Louisville. Archaeological evidence suggests that Indians of the Woodland period explored caves looking for minerals to be used as tools or fashioned into jewelry.

Dramatic changes occurred throughout Kentucky during the Late Prehistoric period (1750 to 1000 B.C.). Corn was introduced to the region and quickly became the most important crop. Beans

Kentucky Mound Builders

The Wickliffe Mounds stand where the Ohio River joins the Mississippi. These mounds consist of two flat-topped, pyramid-shaped earthen structures that were probably places of worship. They were built by Indian people who occupied the land around A.D. 1300. The Mound Builders grew corn and relied on the crop as their staple food. Evidently, they were also great traders. Archaeologists have found articles in the mounds that came from as far north as Wisconsin and as far south as the Gulf of Mexico. The Wickliffe Mounds are administered by Murray State University in Murray, Kentucky. ■

also appeared. Farming gave the early Kentuckians time to build. Working together, they constructed flat-topped earthen mounds that they used as temples. A people called the Mississippians built elaborate mounds in western Kentucky. To the east, a group called the Fort Ancient made decorative pottery.

The Mississippi culture—the great mound-builders—died out for unknown reasons. Most of what is now Kentucky was uninhabited when Europeans established colonies in North America. The region was a hunting ground for several Native American groups such as the Cherokee, the Delaware, and the Shawnee. It was one of the richest hunting grounds in the world.

What did Kentucky look like 300 years ago, before the farmers and the road-builders arrived? Certainly it was a place of stunning beauty. Some of the first English-speaking settlers to see this unspoiled land called it the Eden of the West.

Towering forests covered most of the state. Groves of poplars, hundreds of years old, stood as high as ten-story buildings. The graceful trees measured 10 to 12 feet (3 to 4 m) in diameter at their bases. Water flowed abundantly from countless streams and rivers. The river valleys and forests were home to deer, wild turkeys, and

Kentucky's abundant water was among the resources that drew settlers.

bears; buffalo grazed the prairies in the central part of the state. Some reports say the herds of buffalo in Kentucky were as numerous as those found in the Great Plains far to the west. The rivers teemed with fish. Birds, especially passenger pigeons, flew in flocks so thick that they blocked the sun.

For hunters, the Kentucky of old was a virtual paradise. Even though game animals were plentiful, the Indian tribes fought over hunting territories. And while they battled with one another, a new and more powerful enemy approached the Kentucky forests.

Explorers and Pioneers

Beginning in the 1600s, English immigrants settled along the Atlantic Coast of North America, and French communities emerged farther north in what is now Canada. The French were probably the first Europeans to enter Kentucky. In 1673, the team of Jacques Marquette and Louis Jolliet sailed down the Mississippi River along Kentucky's western tip. Nine years later, the explorer René-Robert Cavelier, Sieur de La Salle, claimed the lands of the Mississippi Valley, including Kentucky, for France. Though these were heroic journeys, the French made little impact on the Kentucky region. The fateful meetings took place between English settlers and Indian cultures.

Jacques Marquette on an expedition along the Mississippi River

By the beginning of the 1700s, the thirteen English colonies were well established in the East. English colonists moved relentlessly west, always seeking new land. But the Appalachian Mountains barred their westward advancement. The great chain of mountains rose like a jagged wall hemming the English into their

John Finley is credited with founding Kentucky.

coastal area. Only the most adventurous colonists were able to pierce this wall and see the amazing lands beyond.

For years, resourceful traders and hunters journeyed west. They canoed down the Ohio River on Kentucky's northern border or they climbed over the Appalachians. One such adventurer was John Finley of Pennsylvania. In 1752, Finley followed the Ohio River to the point where the city of Louisville stands today. Perhaps other hunters whose names have been lost to history also ventured into Kentucky. And perhaps those unnamed hunters found a gateway through the Appalachians long before that passage was officially discovered.

Thomas Walker was a doctor, born in the colony of Virginia. Exploring new lands was one of Dr. Walker's passions. In 1750, he led a party to the western edge of the thirteen colonies. When he encountered the rugged Appalachian Mountains, he trekked along the foothills hoping to find a way to cross the giant peaks. To his

Exploration of Kentucky

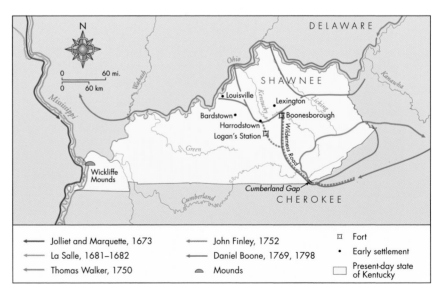

The Cumberland Gap National Historical Park

Today, travelers see the Cumberland Gap in a setting not much different from the land that explorer Dr. Thomas Walker first set foot in. More than 1 million visitors come to the park each year. The Cumberland Gap National Historic Park contains some 18,000 acres (4,290 ha) of wilderness spread out over three states—Kentucky, Virginia, and Tennessee. Miles of scenic hiking trails lead through the gap.

Native Americans had used this mountain pass for thousands of years, and Thomas Walker was probably not the first white man to pass through the valley. But Walker was the first to write about the Cumberland Gap and set the stage for its place in U.S. history. ■

A long hunter in the Kentucky wilderness

astonishment, he discovered a pass that opened like a great door in the mountains. He named the pass the Cumberland Gap in honor of the English duke of Cumberland. In the years to come, the Cumberland Gap became the great gateway to the western United States.

Through the Cumberland Gap passed bands of European long hunters. They were called long hunters because they ventured into the wilderness and stayed for long periods—months, and even years. They emerged with great loads of deerskins and other items to sell in the East. Long hunters in Kentucky saw a wilderness more exciting than anything we can imagine today. They heard the thunder of hoofbeats as hundreds of buffalo raced over the grasslands. The throb of birds in flight sounded like a roaring wind. Of course, the long hunters had to fight Indians, who believed the whites were encroaching on their territory. Sometimes the Indians were content only to rob the strangers. In the late 1760s, a long hunter named Abraham Bledsoe carved an anguished message on a poplar

Harrodstown, the First Outpost

Kentucky's first successful settlement was a village founded by James Harrod. According to most accounts, Pennsylvania-born James Harrod was a perfect frontiersman. He was fearless, tough, and a crack shot with his rifle. In 1774, Harrod and a group of men built a fort and a collection of cabins they called Harrodstown. As the years went by, Harrod became a well-to-do farmer, but he never lost his love for the wilderness. When he was in his fifties, he ventured into the deep forest to hunt and was never seen again. The one-time muddy outpost of Harrodstown is now the city of Harrodsburg in the central part of Kentucky. ■

tree in Kentucky's Wayne County: 2300 DEER
SKINS LOST. RUINATION BY GOD.

Pennsylvania-born Daniel Boone was a
long hunter, an explorer, and a pioneer leader.
He is also one of the great names in Kentucky history. In 1769, Boone set out with his
friend John Finley, who had journeyed earlier
across the Ohio River. Boone wanted to go
through the Cumberland Gap and see the
fabulous land easterners were beginning to
call "Kaintuck." Beyond the mountains,
Boone discovered fertile soil and more game
animals than he had ever seen before. He
called the place a "terrestrial paradise." In
1775, Boone and a group of farmers built a
fort on the Kentucky River just south of present-day Lexington. The settlement came to
be called Boonesborough.

**Daniel Boone being
captured by the
Shawnee Indians**

From the beginning, Boone and his followers clashed with the
Indians. One day in 1778, Shawnee warriors captured Boone and
about thirty other men as they hunted near the fort. The Shawnee
formed two lines and made the captives run between them while
they rained blows on the men with their war clubs. Boone took his
turn "running the gauntlet." At the end of the two lines he saw a
huge Shawnee brave standing firmly to block his exit. Boone lowered his head like a football player, knocked the man down, and
jumped over him. The Shawnee admired Boone's courage and

Jemima Boone, Hero of the Kentucky Frontier

Daniel Boone's wife, Rebecca, and his daughter, Jemima, traveled with him when Boonesborough was founded. They were the first white women to settle on the Kentucky frontier. In July 1776, fourteen-year-old Jemima and two of her friends were canoeing on the Kentucky River when they were surprised and captured by Shawnee warriors. The Shawnee led them to a forest camp where they hoped to hold the girls for ransom. Along the way, Jemima secretly tore off bits of her dress and tied them to tree branches. Jemima reasoned her sharp-eyed father would be able to follow the trail she left. Aided by the bits of cloth, Daniel Boone discovered the camp and rescued the girls. For generations, frontier families told and retold the story of Jemima Boone's cool-headed courage in the face of mortal danger. ■

invited him to join their tribe. Boone befriended the Shawnee long enough to gain their confidence. Then he escaped.

Boone had other dangerous and tragic fights with Kentucky Indians. About three years before the founding of Boonesborough, a scouting party that Boone sent to Kentucky was attacked and overwhelmed by Indian warriors. Boone's twelve-year-old son and one of his men were captured and tortured to death. Despite his son's terrible ordeal, Boone never harbored hatred toward the Indians. He had grown up a Quaker, a religion that strongly values peacefulness. All his life he condemned violence and warfare. Over the years Boone became close friends with many Indians. He learned and respected the Native American ways of life.

"The Dark and Bloody Ground"

In the half-dozen years following the founding of Boonesborough, about 12,000 settlers trekked through the Cumberland Gap to enter Kentucky. They marched into peril. The Revolutionary War (1775–1783) broke out between England and its American colonies in 1775 and raged for eight years. The biggest battles took place in the East. In Kentucky, British agents armed Indians and encouraged them to attack settlements. The Indians, who believed the settlers were taking land they had owned for hundreds of years, fought with desperate ferocity. The meaning of the Indian word for Kentucky as "dark and bloody ground" fell with its full horror on the settlers.

Pioneer Kentucky farmers working in fields were constantly on the lookout for Indian raiding parties. At the first sign of trouble the fastest runner—often a teenaged boy—was sent to warn families

A Native American raid at Logan's Station

in neighboring cabins. Then everyone took shelter in the community fort. The forts were log blockhouses that kept invaders out, but they also trapped the defenders inside. A terrible kind of siege warfare broke out in Kentucky. Bands of warriors surrounded forts, hoping to starve the settlers out. While standing guard outside the walls, the Indians shrieked war whoops. Hunger, thirst, and fear were key weapons in these brutal battles.

The year 1777 was called the Year of the Bloody Sevens by frontier Kentuckians. Just about every community was raided, and horror spread throughout the settlements. A Kentucky fort called Logan's Station (near the present-day city of Stanford) was besieged for thirteen days in 1777. At one point, the fort's starving inhabitants attempted to go beyond the walls to milk some cows in a pasture. The milking expedition was led by Ann Logan, Mrs. William Whitley, and an unnamed slave woman. The Indians opened fire, and one of the men guarding the milkers was wounded. He was later rescued by other men who rushed out of the fort using the mattress of a featherbed as a shield against Indian arrows.

In 1778, Boonesborough was attacked by as many as 450 Shawnee. They surrounded the fort and shot at defenders who dared poke their heads above the walls. Each side used tricks to break down its opponent's will to fight. The Shawnee fired flaming arrows into Boonesborough's walls. When that tactic failed, the Indians attempted to tunnel under the ground to enter the fort. Daniel Boone, who had recently escaped from the Shawnee, hit upon the idea of filling a hollowed-out log with powder and shot and using it as a cannon. The trick worked once, but the second time the log blew up in the defenders' hands. The Shawnee withdrew after a ten-day siege. Miraculously, only two defenders were killed.

Mrs. John Merrell is remembered for her bravery against the Shawnee.

Kentucky women became legendary fighters during the war years. One night in 1787, a Nelson County cabin owned by Mr. and Mrs. John Merrell was attacked before the family could flee to the fort. John Merrell was shot and wounded at the cabin door. His wife found an ax in the darkness. Standing over the

Blue Licks Battlefield State Park.
The 1782 battle that cost Daniel Boone's son Israel his life was fought at a spot called Blue Licks. Today the Blue Licks Battlefield State Park honors those who fell. A monument in the park contains Daniel Boone's tribute to the Kentuckians who died there: ENOUGH OF HONOR CANNOT BE PAID. ■

unconscious body of her husband, she killed four Shawnee as they tried to burst through the smashed cabin door. Then she heard two more Indians attempting to come down the chimney. Mrs. Merrell smoked them out by setting pillows on fire and pushing them into the fireplace. Others in the raiding band fled.

Kentucky's bloodiest Revolutionary War battle took place on August 19, 1782, near the present-day city of Mount Olivet. At Licking River, about 200 mounted Kentucky militiamen intercepted a much larger band of British-led Indians. Daniel Boone was one of the militia leaders. Boone and other experienced soldiers cautioned against attacking because they were outnumbered at least three to one. But the will of younger, hot-headed officers prevailed, and the horse-mounted militia charged. In only fifteen minutes, some sixty Kentuckians were killed. Boone escaped by swimming the river. His son Israel Boone was among those slain in the fighting.

The Battle of Blue Licks was a disaster for Kentuckians, but it was the final significant Revolutionary War battle fought on Ken-

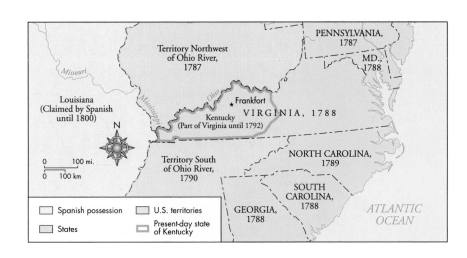

tucky soil. It was also the state's last important clash with Indians, although skirmishes broke out for decades.

The Revolutionary War ended in 1783 and a new nation—the United States of America—was created. The nation's borders stretched from the Atlantic Ocean to the Mississippi River. Yet two out of every three people in the United States still lived within 50 miles (80 km) of the Atlantic coast. This would change in the 1800s as men and women from the East traveled westward and created new states in their path. Kentucky was the first state formed west of the mountains. The 1800s could be called its first century.

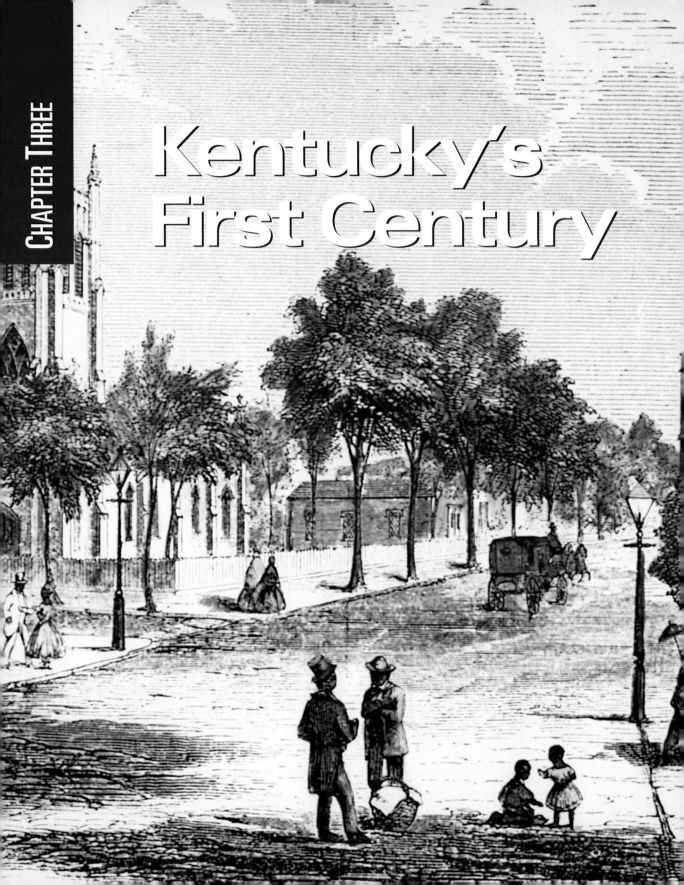

CHAPTER THREE

Kentucky's First Century

Kentucky statesman Henry Clay once rode over a lonely path toward a mountain community. At the Cumberland Gap he stopped his horse and sat silently as if listening to something. His companion asked why he had paused. He said, "I am listening to the tread of the coming millions." Though Clay heard nothing at that moment, his statement was correct. Millions of settlers poured through the Cumberland Gap to begin new lives in the West. In the early 1800s, the land between the Appalachian Mountains and the Mississippi River was considered the United States' western frontier. Kentucky was the gateway to the West.

Floating down the Ohio River

Settlers and Statehood

Kentucky had two major avenues that invited pioneer families westward. One was the Cumberland Gap, which people crossed on foot. Settlers usually took farm animals—pigs, cows, and chickens—with them. The path beyond the gap was called the Wilderness Road.

The Ohio River, which flows along Kentucky's northern border, was a second great highway to the western frontier. Farm families

Opposite: Louisville in the 1850s

floated downriver on log rafts called flatboats, or Kentucky flats. Their decks crowded with animals, the flatboats streamed down the Ohio amid a chorus of neighing horses, mooing cows, and barking dogs. One Ohio River traveler said, "It is no uncommon spectacle to see [on flatboats] a large family [plus] cattle, hogs, horses, sheep, fowls, and animals of all kinds bringing to recollection the cargo of the ancient [Noah's] ark."

Many families traveled through Kentucky on their way to other parts of the western frontier. Kentucky was the final destination for thousands. By the time the Revolutionary War ended, there were 30,000 settlers in Kentucky. Cities such as Louisville (founded in 1778) and Lexington (1779) were already expanding.

New Kentucky residents came from every part of the East. The majority of the newcomers, however, heralded from Virginia, Pennsylvania, North Carolina, and Maryland. A swelling population meant that Kentucky had enough people to become a state. Early in the nation's history, the original thirteen colonies claimed land in the western frontier. Thus Kentucky was still considered to be an extension of Virginia. Virginia yielded its claim, and in 1792 Kentucky was admitted to the United States as the fifteenth state. Frankfort was chosen as the state capital. Frankfort's most prominent resident, Andrew Holmes, gave the state free land, the use of a warehouse, and several horses and cows as an incentive to establish the capital there.

Kentucky's first constitution was adopted in 1792 in the city of Danville. Framers of that constitution struggled with the issue of slavery. Black slaves had been in Kentucky since its infancy. They accompanied the explorers who probed the West in the 1750s.

Frankfort was chosen as Kentucky's capital in 1792.

Slaves were at Boonesborough and most of the other forts. They fought side by side with whites against Indian raiders. Still, the Kentucky constitution made slavery a legal institution. The constitution included this measure although slavery was dying in the northern states even in the 1790s. Kentucky was a border state, neither northern nor southern. Many Kentuckians were transplanted southerners who believed they had a God-given right to own slaves. That right, they believed, could not be taken away by laws or by state constitutions.

Monk Estill

Monk Estill was a slave in early Kentucky. He lived with his master, James Estill, in a fort called Estill's Station, near present-day Richmond. Monk Estill was an important man in the fort because he was especially skilled in mixing gunpowder. In 1782, Monk Estill and several other settlers were captured by Wyandot Indians. The Wyandots wanted to assault Fort Estill, but Monk told them it was defended by more than one hundred well-armed men. Actually, the fort had only a few dozen defenders. Monk Estill's exaggerated report convinced the Wynandots not to attack and thus saved the settlers inside the fort. As a reward for his heroism Monk Estill was given his freedom. He was probably the first slave in Kentucky to be freed. ■

Life of the Pioneers

The pioneers streaming into Kentucky were experienced farmers with an eye for good soil. In the wilds, they staked out claims and cleared land they believed would become productive farmland. Most of the land in Kentucky was owned by the federal government. The government, eager to develop the western frontier, sold the land for less than $1 per acre (0.4 ha), and the settler had three years to pay.

The western pioneers had a genius for transforming the wilderness into comfortable communities. Trekking across the rugged Appalachians meant they could bring few goods with them. Therefore, once they settled in Kentucky, their houses—and everything they ate and wore—were the products of their own hands.

In heavily wooded Kentucky, log-cabin communities popped up everywhere in the early 1800s. Working together, a dozen men and women put up a log cabin in less than a week. Nails were not used in construction because nails and other iron products were rare in the West. For the first year or so, the bare ground served as the cabin's floor. Eventually, the pioneer family installed a floor made of split logs with the flat sides up. As a further improvement, a family might build a second floor, or loft, just below the cabin's slanted roof. Boys usually slept in the loft, and it was called the boys' room.

Corn was the pioneer's most important crop. A plate piled high with corn bread was served at practically every meal. Hogs provided meat for the pioneers. And just about every cabin kept chickens. Wild game remained an

Many Kentucky homes were log cabins.

Abraham Lincoln, the Log-Cabin President

Abraham Lincoln, the sixteenth president of the United States, was born on February 12, 1809, in a log cabin near the present-day city of Hodgenville. Visitors at Hodgenville's Abraham Lincoln Birthplace National Historic Site examine a nineteenth-century log cabin, that resembles one in which Lincoln was born.

When he was seven years old, Lincoln and his family moved to Indiana and eventually to Illinois. Much has been written about Lincoln's humble beginnings in a Kentucky log cabin. But Lincoln never considered his childhood to be impoverished. Log-cabin villages housed small farmers, the working class of the times. ■

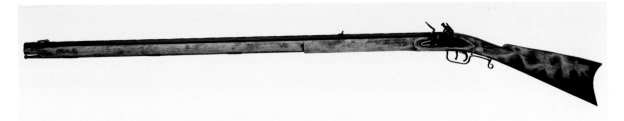

The "Kentucky Rifle"

Hunting was not a sport in pioneer Kentucky. People hunted to feed their families. Most hunters were armed with the "Kentucky Rifle," praised throughout the West for its accuracy. The rifle was created by Pennsylvania gunsmiths and modified by Kentuckians. Mostly the Kentuckians lengthened the barrel to about 45 inches (114 cm). The longer barrel gave the rifle its precision, but it made the rifle almost as long as the man carrying it. ■

important source of food. A deer killed by a hunter could feed a family for many days. Tobacco was an early cash crop for western Kentucky. Western Kentucky had many streams that connected to the Ohio and Mississippi Rivers. Farmers there were able to ship their tobacco to markets in New Orleans.

A camp meeting in the early 1800s

Frontier living was harsh, but early Kentuckians enjoyed getting together to dance, sing, or worship. Of all frontier activities nothing equaled the excitement of outdoor church services, called camp meetings. The services were conducted by preachers who traveled from one village to another. In the early 1800s, these preachers fanned the flames of the Great Revival, a religious movement that swept the West. At meetings, men and women prayed with such passion that they seemed to lose their senses. Possessed with spiritual energy, they danced, rolled on the ground, or barked like dogs. A famous 1801 camp meeting held at Cane Ridge in Kentucky's Bourbon County drew more than 20,000 worshipers, many of whom went into convulsions during the fervor of mass prayer.

Pioneer Kentuckians also partied with an almost religious zeal. The completion of a log cabin called for feasting, music, and dance. At cornhusking parties, young people formed teams and tried to be first to fill a barrel with corn stripped of its leaves. According to tradition, a young man who husked a rare red ear of

A Kentucky wedding meant a big celebration.

Clay and the War Hawks

Kentuckians and most people of the western frontier favored a second war with England. The pioneers believed the British were encouraging Indian attacks on settlements in the West. Western congressmen, led by Henry Clay (left), formed a group called the War Hawks because of their lust for war. When the War of 1812 (1812-1815) broke out with England, some Americans dubbed it Mr. Clay's War. During the war some 1,200 Kentucky soldiers fought with General Andrew Jackson at the 1815 Battle of New Orleans. A ballad, which was popular in the 1820s, celebrated the Kentuckians' courage:

Jackson he was wide awake,
And wasn't scar'd of trifles.
For well he knew what aim we'd
take
With our Kentucky rifles. ■

corn was allowed to kiss the young woman on his right. A frontier wedding was the biggest bash of all. During wedding celebrations, the host loaded tables with food. Most male party-goers guzzled homemade corn liquor, often with disastrous results. Home-brewed whiskey smelled terrible, tasted worse than it smelled, and just half a jug of it made a person crazy drunk. Frontier parties frequently ended in bloody brawls.

Though they represented a young state, Kentucky politicians were national leaders in the 1800s. The most famous Kentucky politician was Henry Clay. Born in Virginia, Clay moved to Kentucky at an early age and won his first election there in 1803. He remained in Kentucky politics for forty years. Outspoken and hot-tempered, he fought several duels with political opponents. He ran for president of the United States three times but never won. Always he championed issues he thought were

Covington in the 1850s

right. Clay is famous for his statement "I had rather be right than be President."

The 1820 census counted more than half a million people living in Kentucky, making it the nation's sixth most populous state. Tiny farm communities became thriving cities. Bowling Green (founded in 1798) grew as a river port. Hopkinsville (incorporated in 1804) expanded as a market center. Covington was created in 1815, and that same year Owensboro was chosen as the county seat for Daviess County.

Rivers: The Highways of Early Kentucky

In the early 1800s, people and goods moved through Kentucky on riverboats. The first such craft were log rafts called flatboats.

Flatboats were rowed or poled through rivers by rough, hard-drinking men who described themselves as "half horse, half alligator, and half snapping turtle." In 1811, the first steamboat appeared on the Ohio River, ushering in a new era for river transportation. Louisville became the Ohio River's busiest shipping port.

Other Kentucky cities on the Ohio and its tributaries also benefited from riverboat commerce. Ashland, Beattyville, Bowling Green, Carrollton, Covington, Newport, and Paducah all grew through riverboat commerce. ■

As Kentucky enjoyed spectacular growth, the United States was torn apart by the explosive issue of slavery. President Thomas Jefferson once said slavery harkened and alarmed the nation, "like a fire bell in the night."

Slavery and War

In 1818, a traveler named H. B. Fearon passed through the Kentucky village of Middletown. Behind a tavern, he heard the screams of a young boy. He saw two men taking turns beating a naked fourteen-year-old slave boy with a horsewhip. Fearon asked what the boy had done to deserve such punishment. He was told the whipping was due to the boy's "refusal to cut wood."

By 1850, the state's population approached 1 million, and almost one in four Kentuckians were slaves. Many white Kentuckians said—with pride—that they treated slaves as if they were members of their own family. But generally a slave's life was one of toil, harsh punishments, and fear. Slaves lived in tiny cabins behind the master's house. Slave families could be split up and sold at the will of the owner. As dismal as life was for Kentucky slaves, they dreaded being "sold down the river," meaning being sold farther south. Conditions for slaves in the far southern states were even worse than in Kentucky. And living in the far South made it more difficult to escape to the North and possibly find a new life.

Crossing the Ohio River to the North was the first step to freedom for an escaping Kentucky slave. Henry Bibb, from Shelby County, was Kentucky's most daring escape artist. In 1837, Bibb broke away from his owner and swam across the river to Ohio. When he returned to try to free his wife, he was recaptured. He escaped twice more, only to be caught again while attempting to reach his wife in Kentucky. Bibb finally won his freedom and wrote a popular book titled *Adventures of Henry Bibb, an American Slave.*

Uncle Tom's Cabin

It is believed that Harriet Beecher Stowe, an Ohio resident, once visited friends in the town of Washington, Kentucky. There she witnessed a slave auction on the courthouse steps. Families were torn apart as individuals were sold to far-flung farms. She saw the slaves' grief and heard their desperate weeping.

The scene moved Stowe to write her powerful antislavery novel *Uncle Tom's Cabin*. The novel contains a riveting escape scene when the heroine, Eliza, races over the ice-choked Ohio River with her baby in her arms. Published in 1852, the book stirred such strong antislavery sentiments that Southern states forbade people to have it in their homes. ■

In 1848, about fifty-five slaves attempted a mass escape from farms near Lexington. Somehow the slaves had managed to get rifles. A gun battle broke out between the slaves and the state militia. Most of the slaves were recaptured. The 1848 Kentucky uprising was one of the largest slave revolts in U.S. history.

Many Kentuckians denounced slavery and urged the state and the nation to abolish it. One fiery abolitionist was Cassius Marcellus Clay, a cousin of Henry Clay. In Lexington, Cassius Clay operated an antislavery newspaper. The paper infuriated Clay's slaveholding neighbors. A Lexington man once hired an assassin to shoot Clay. But Clay, a ferocious fighter, managed to attack the gunman and wound him with a knife. Clay campaigned for Abraham Lincoln in the election of 1860 and later served in Lincoln's administration.

Lincoln's election as president in 1860 inflamed the nation. Before Lincoln took office, seven Southern states had broken away from the country. Four others followed, and together they formed the Confederate States of America. On April 12, 1861, Confederate cannons bombarded Fort Sumter, a military base in Charleston, South Carolina. The bloody American Civil War began.

For four years, U.S. citizens fought, brother against brother. At the beginning of the conflict, the Kentucky legislature declared itself neutral. Kentucky was a border state, bitterly divided between Northern and Southern sympathies. Many of its residents were pro-slavery, but just as many wanted to keep the United States together as one nation. Being neutral allowed Kentuckians to fight on either side. Some 75,000 Kentucky men chose to fight for the North, and about 35,000 fought for the South. The prominent family of Henry Clay served as an example of Kentucky's divided loyalties. Clay died in 1852, leaving five grandsons. Two of his grandsons joined the forces of the North, while three fought for the South.

In 1863, President Lincoln allowed blacks to join the Northern army. In return for their service, Lincoln promised to give them freedom for themselves and for their wives and children. Some 28,000 Kentucky slaves answered Lincoln's call and joined the

Cassius Clay worked hard to end slavery.

Kentucky: One Foot in the North, the Other Foot in the South

Many curious coincidences marked Kentucky as a state with loyalties on both sides of the Civil War. Jefferson Davis (right), the leader of the Confederate states, was born in Kentucky. Davis's birthplace was just 100 miles (161 km) from that of Abraham Lincoln. Mary Todd Lincoln, the wife of Abraham Lincoln, was born into a wealthy Kentucky family that owned slaves. Southern general John Hunt Morgan, known as "The Thunderbolt of the Confederacy" was also a Kentuckian. ■

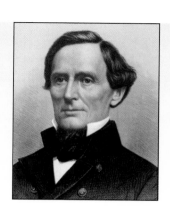

Northern ranks. Many of these slaves had simply walked away from their frustrated masters to enter the army. The Civil War ended in April 1865. In December of that year, the Thirteenth Amendment to the U.S. Constitution officially freed all the nation's slaves.

After the Civil War, Kentucky enjoyed a period of industrial expansion. Industrial employment increased 200 percent in the

The Battle of Perryville

Kentucky's deadliest battle of the American Civil War took place near Perryville on October 8, 1862. Northern and Southern armed forces met outside the town almost by accident, as both sides sought water.

In an incredible flurry of cannon and rifle fire, about 1,600 men were killed and 5,400 wounded in just four hours. Neither side emerged a clear victor, but the Southern forces were forced to retreat. The 250-acre (101 ha) Perryville Battlefield State Historic Site commemorates the battle. ■

years between 1870 and 1900. The state's railroads expanded three-fold in the same period. Tobacco was still the most important cash crop. And coal fed the furnaces of the nation. The distilling of whiskey became a major industry. Later historians would sadly note that two of Kentucky's major industries—tobacco and whiskey—ruined the health of millions who used those products to excess.

Preparing a cargo of tobacco in Louisville

Aristides, the Game Little Colt

The first Kentucky Derby in 1875 was won by a golden-red, three-year-old colt called Aristides. His jockey was an African-American named Oliver Lewis. Some 12,000 spectators came to the brand new Churchill Downs race track to watch that first Kentucky Derby. Aristides, who was small by racehorse standards, later ran in Baltimore and New York, where he broke several long-standing speed records. ■

Horse breeding was a glamour industry that blossomed after the Civil War. For years, Thoroughbred horses had been raised on farms in the rolling hills near Lexington. This is the heart of the Bluegrass Region, ideal grounds for horses. In 1875, a banker named Lewis Clark built a racecourse near Louisville. He named the racecourse Churchill Downs, after two of his uncles. Clark then put on a grand race called the Kentucky Derby. Thus, a tradition was born. Horse breeding and horse racing became symbols of Kentucky for generations to come.

CHAPTER FOUR

Twentieth-Century Kentucky

A tobacco farmer being watched by an armed guard during the Black Patch War

The dynamic growth Kentucky enjoyed in the 1800s tapered off in the twentieth century. Kentucky's industrial development began to lag behind that of other states. Many people left Kentucky to find better job opportunities elsewhere. Between 1950 and 1990, Kentucky's population registered a 30 percent increase, while the nation's population as a whole grew almost 70 percent. Still, love of home remained the theme of the Kentucky story. Though job-seeking men and women migrated to other states, they thought of Kentucky as their true home.

Strife!

In 1899, William S. Taylor ran for governor of Kentucky against William Goebel. The campaign was ugly. Each candidate accused the other of lying and corruption. William Taylor won the election by a very small margin. Goebel's supporters cried "vote fraud" and demanded a recount. Then, on January 30, 1900, Goebel was shot on the road to Frankfort. He died four days later. The assassination threw Kentucky into a virtual civil war. Arguments between political backers escalated from fistfights to shootings.

Strife in politics, on the farms, and in the coal mines was a grim chapter of the Kentucky story in the early twentieth century. Unrest on the farms exploded into what was called the Black Patch War. The Black Patch is a tobacco-growing region in western Kentucky.

Opposite: The Louisville Slugger bat factory

Madeline Breckinridge (1872–1920)

In a time of labor wars and violent politics, a woman of peace and progress grew up in Kentucky. Madeline Breckinridge was the great-granddaughter of Henry Clay. She was a crusader for voting rights at a time when women were not allowed to vote. Breckinridge was also a social worker devoted to bringing educational opportunities to poor children. A powerful public speaker, she often said that only when women had the vote would politicians respond to their needs. Breckinridge died in 1920, just before the adoption of the Nineteenth Amendment to the U.S. Constitution. That amendment granted voting privileges to U.S. women. ■

In 1904, tobacco farmers of the Black Patch met in the town of Guthrie. The farmers agreed to keep their tobacco in warehouses rather than sell it for the low prices offered by the giant American Tobacco Company. The American Tobacco Company countered by giving higher prices to any farmer who would defy the will of the Guthrie Meeting and sell tobacco. Farmers who sold their tobacco were then attacked by enraged neighbors. Crops were burned and farmers who made deals with the American Tobacco Company were beaten up. For almost four years the Black Patch War spread terror in western Kentucky. Raiders set fire to company ware-houses in Trenton, Princeton, and Hopkinsville.

In 1917 and 1918, U.S. involvement in World War I (1914–1918) temporarily ended the labor conflicts sweeping the state. Wartime demand increased the prices of Kentucky farm goods and coal, and some 75,000 Kentuckians served in the armed forces. Camp Knox (later Fort Knox) became an important army training base. But immediately after the war, strife returned to Kentucky. This time violence struck in the eastern Kentucky coal region.

Coal miners worked twelve-hour shifts in dark tunnels, some-times knee-deep in water. They breathed coal dust until they

Coal miners worked long hours in very difficult conditions.

coughed up blood. Always, they risked the horror of a cave-in. Despite these wretched working conditions, coal miners had to accept low wages. Coal is a boom or bust industry. Most of the 1920s and the 1930s were bust years as the price of coal dropped. Labor unions tried to organize the miners, but coal company bosses sometimes used a private police force to bully—and sometimes even murder—pro-union miners. In the early 1930s, Kentucky's Harlan County was known as Bloody Harlan because of constant labor skirmishes.

The Great Depression of the 1930s brought suffering and unemployment to the United States—and to Kentucky. Nationally, one in every four people lost their jobs. In Kentucky, the jobless figure was even higher. Many businesspeople refused to open factories and shops in Kentucky because they saw it as a state prone to labor violence. By 1940, Kentucky ranked lowest among the states in individual income.

Simon B. Buckner, Kentucky Hero

Leading the Tenth Army at the bloody Battle of Okinawa was General Simon B. Buckner. Born in Hart County, his father served as governor of Kentucky from 1887 to 1891. The general's hunger for victory over the Japanese was legend. Buckner's favorite wartime toast was, "May you walk in the ashes of Tokyo." On June 18, 1945, just two months before the war ended, Buckner inspected a forward area on Okinawa. An enemy shell struck, and he was killed. General Simon B. Buckner was the highest-ranking U.S. officer killed on a fighting front during World War II. He now lies in the Frankfort cemetery. ▪

New Beginnings

Despite the troubling times, Kentuckians rallied to their country's call during World War II (1939–1945). In 1941, the United States joined the Allied forces against Germany, Italy, and Japan. More than 300,000 Kentucky men and women served in the armed forces. Seven Kentuckians won the Congressional Medal of Honor, the nation's highest award for bravery. Thousands of troops trained at Fort Knox and at Camp Breckinridge near Morganfield. On the home front, the state's coal mines and factories worked at a dizzying pace. Nearly 100,000 jeeps rolled out of Louisville's Ford Motor Company. A huge ammunition plant at Paducah employed hundreds of people in round-the-clock shifts.

The Louisville Ford Motor Company Plant produced jeeps during World War II.

World War II opened up job opportunities to Kentucky's blacks and women. After the war, thousands of returning soldiers, even those from impoverished families, chose to attend college. African-Americans would no longer accept discrimination. All Kentuckians became concerned about pollution and industrial development ruining the natural beauty of their state. The postwar years were troubling but exciting times in Kentucky.

Signs saying COLORED WAITING ROOM and WHITE WAITING ROOM once greeted train travelers throughout the South, including Ken-

Separate water fountains for "whites" and "coloreds"

FOR COLORED ONLY

tucky. Racial segregation was the law of the land. Black children attended a separate school system. Restaurants and lunch counters were segregated. Movie houses had "white" and "colored" sections. Even public drinking fountains were separate.

For generations, black Kentuckians had fought the state's segregationist laws. The blacks enjoyed little success until the 1940s, when changes came first in education. In 1948, the University of Kentucky began accepting black students. Then, in 1954, the U.S. Supreme Court declared that school segregation of any kind violated the U.S. Constitution. Shortly after the Supreme Court's decision, Kentucky governor Lawrence Wetherby announced he would obey the new law. Thus Kentucky became the first border state or southern state to integrate its school system.

In the 1960s, Kentucky and the South were the scene of demonstrations and civil rights marches. Slowly the laws of the past faded. A state civil rights law, passed in 1966, banned discrimination in public facilities. Martin Luther King Jr. called the 1966 Kentucky law, "the strongest and most comprehensive civil rights bill passed by a southern state." After passage of the law, most Kentucky restaurants and other public facilities integrated with few problems. The South was changing, and Kentucky led the forces of change.

In eastern Kentucky, citizens looked with alarm at developments in the coalfields. The eastern Kentucky mountains are among the most wildly beautiful regions in this very beautiful state. But a coal-extraction process called strip-mining uprooted forests, leveled mountains, and polluted streams. In 1966, Kentucky wrote the nation's toughest strip-mining law. The law required mining com-

Strip-Mining, the Scourge of the Environment

Coal is found in seams in mountains, resembling layers in a cake. Tunneling into a seam and digging out the coal is one method of mining. Strip-mining is a faster, cheaper, and safer process. A strip-mining operation uses giant shovels that strip away the top of a mountain to expose the layer of coal. Smaller shovels then dig out the coal and load it on trucks. Strip mining, though efficient, leaves the top of a mountain barren and also scars the land where the waste material is dumped. All strip-mining operations are now carefully regulated in Kentucky. ■

A young man being arrested during racial demonstrations in Louisville, 1961

panies to repair all the damage caused by strip-mining. Such repairs included restoring soil and replanting trees. A later strip-mining law passed by the federal government was modeled after the Kentucky legislation.

Kentucky Today

An oil shortage in the early 1970s renewed the nation's interest in coal as a prime source of power. Kentucky was one of the country's

Martha Layne Collins, Kentucky's first female governor, was elected in 1983.

leading coal-producing states. Wages in the coalfields had increased dramatically since the violent days of the Harlan County strikes. But the coal-mining process became more automated. Machines now dug out most of the coal, and miners found limited job opportunities. Kentucky's coal regions remained some of the poorest sections of the state.

In 1979, Kentuckians chose John Y. Brown as their governor. Years earlier, Brown had bought into the Kentucky Fried Chicken chain, which sold chicken prepared by a "secret formula of herbs and spices." The fried-chicken franchise made Brown a millionaire. In office, he promised to run the state efficiently, as he had his fried-chicken business. Kentuckians elected their first woman governor, Martha Layne Collins, in 1983. A former high-school teacher, she fought hard to increase funds for the state's school system.

A band played and dignitaries gathered in 1988 when the Toyota Motor Company opened an $800-million assembly plant at Georgetown, which is just north of Lexington. At first the plant employed 3,000 workers and turned out 200,000 cars a year. Production figures quickly increased after the plant's first few years of operation. More than 200 other Kentucky firms were contracted to supply parts for the giant auto factory. Including the supporting shops, the Georgetown car-building operation generated 10,000 to 15,000 jobs for the state.

Kentucky faced a school crisis in 1988 when the state supreme court ruled that the school system violated the state constitution. The court held that schools in rich neighborhoods got more funds than schools in poor communities. Other reports claimed that one-third of all Kentuckians had failed to complete high school and that the amount of money the state spent on schools ranked forty-first among the fifty states. The Kentucky government responded to this alarming situation by passing the Education Reform Act of 1990. The act reorganized school systems and set new goals for students. Between 1990 and 1995, the state increased funding for education by 46.5 percent. By 1995, the Kentucky school system's ranking in per-pupil expenditure had risen to twenty-first place among the states.

As the 1990s came to a close, the state looked to improved education and growing industrial jobs as a key to progress. Most Kentuckians approached the twenty-first century with confidence.

CHAPTER FIVE

Treasures of the Land

Certainly, one of the reasons Kentuckians love their home state is because of the land's stunning beauty. Few other states are blessed with such diverse scenery. Kentucky has towering mountains, rushing streams, rolling grasslands, and pleasant meadows. Visitors are overwhelmed by this state, and Kentuckians living elsewhere always long for home.

Kentucky's landscape is diverse and often breathtaking.

Geography and Land Regions

Kentucky is truly a border state. Its people are not quite northern; nor are they fully southern in their attitudes and ways of life. Other border states include Tennessee and West Virginia. Some

Opposite: Cumberland Falls State Park

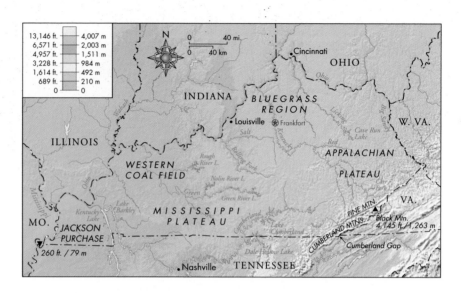

Kentucky's topography

geographers classify Delaware, Maryland, Virginia, and North Carolina as border states.

In terms of land area, Kentucky ranks thirty-seventh among the fifty states. Its two major defining features are the Appalachian Mountains in the east and the Ohio River in the north. The Appalachian Mountains form Kentucky's eastern border with West Virginia and Virginia. The Ohio River makes up the northern border with Ohio, Illinois, and Indiana. At the state's western tip, the Mississippi River separates Kentucky from Missouri. In the south, a human-made line serves as the boundary with Tennessee.

Geologists divide Kentucky into five major land regions: the Appalachian Plateau, the Bluegrass Region, the Mississippi Plateau, the Western Coal Field, and the Jackson Purchase. The divisions are based on the land features and on the type of vegetation and climate.

Black Mountain, Giant of the Cumberlands

Kentucky's portion of the Appalachians is a chain called the Cumberland Mountains. The highest of the Cumberlands— and the highest point in Kentucky—is Black Mountain, which rises 4,139 feet (1,262 m) above sea level. ■

The Appalachian Plateau, the mountainous area of eastern Kentucky, is made up primarily of the Cumberland Mountains. Black Mountain, in the Cumberlands, is the highest point in the state. Also in the Appalachian Plateau is the famous Cumberland Gap, the Gateway to the West in U.S. history. Most of the state's coal is mined in the Appalachian Plateau.

A blue mist rises off the grass in the Bluegrass Region.

The Bluegrass Region is in the center of the state, with the city of Lexington its focus. Gently rolling hills covered with grasses are characteristic of the area. Before the settlers came, huge herds of buffalo grazed here. The area is now home to the swiftest horses in the world.

The Mississippi Plateau lies below the Bluegrass Region and spreads to the Tennessee border. This area is sometimes called the Pennyroyal Region, after a mint that grows in its soil. A stretch of land the early settlers called the Barrens, because it was relatively treeless, lies in the south. The settlers soon discovered the land they had dismissed as "barren" was rich and fertile.

The Western Coal Field is a semicircular area extending south of the Ohio River. It has rocky hills, especially in its southern portions. About one-fourth of the state's coal production is concentrated here, giving the region its name. Oil and natural gas are also taken from the ground. The Western Coal Field is relatively small, consisting of about 4,200 square miles (10,878 sq km).

The Jackson Purchase region rests on the state's western tip. It is called the Jackson Purchase because it is part of the large land area Andrew Jackson (later president of the United States) bought from Indians in 1818. Swamps and small ponds are common in the area. Corn and soybeans are important crops. Kentucky's lowest elevation (257 feet [78 m] above sea level) is found here, in Fulton County along the Mississippi River.

The Kentucky River is among the state's major rivers.

Rivers, Lakes, and Climate

Kentucky is well watered. It receives a total precipitation (a combination of rain and melted snow) measuring 47 inches (119 cm) a year. Compare this figure with Ohio, Kentucky's northern neighbor. Ohio averages 37 inches (94 cm) of total precipitation annually. Spring is the rainiest time of year in Kentucky. The southern half of the state receives slightly more rain than does the north.

All this rain, of course, produces many rivers. The state has more than 13,000 miles

(20,917 km) of rivers and streams. The Green River, Kentucky's longest river, runs within the state. Other major rivers within the state include the Licking, the Kentucky, and the Cumberland.

The mountainous terrain found in many parts of the state creates rapid-flowing streams and waterfalls. Kentucky has more miles of rushing rivers than any other state except Alaska. For this reason white-water rafting has long been popular. The state's largest waterfall is the Cumberland Falls on the Cumberland River near the city of Corbin. At 68 feet (21 m) in height, the Cumberland Falls is the second-tallest waterfall east of the Rocky Mountains.

Despite its wealth of rain and rivers, Kentucky has few sizable lakes. In fact, almost all of its large lakes were artificially created

Cumberland Falls is the state's tallest waterfall.

Kentucky's Geographical Features

Total area; rank	40,411 sq. mi. (104,665 sq km), 37th
Land; rank	39,732 sq. mi. (102,906 sq km), 36th
Water; rank	679 sq. mi. (1,759 sq km), 37th
Inland water; **rank**	679 sq. mi. (1,759 sq km), 32nd
Geographic center	Marion, 3 miles (5 km) northwest of Lebanon
Highest point	Black Mountain, 4,139 feet (1,262 m)
Lowest point	At the Mississippi River, 257 feet (78 m)
Largest city	Louisville
Population; rank	3,698,969 (1990 census); 23rd
Record high temperature	114°F (46°C) at Greensburg on July 28, 1930
Record low temperature	–34°F (–37°C) at Cynthiana on January 28, 1963
Average July temperature	77°F (25°C)
Average January temperature	34°F (1°C)
Average annual precipitation	47 inches (119 cm)

by damming rivers and allowing the waters to fill a valley. Kentucky Lake was built in this manner in 1944. At that time, Kentucky Lake was the largest man-made lake in the world; it is now the second largest in the state. Lake Cumberland, created in 1952, is the state's largest lake. Other substantial lakes, all of which are man-made, include Rough River Lake, Nolin Lake, Lake Barkley, and Carr Fork Lake.

Kentucky enjoys a gentle climate most of the year, but it can get hot and humid in the summer. During the hot spells, the upland regions in the east stay relatively pleasant while people in the south and west swelter. Winters tend to be mild. In Lexington the

Kentucky's climate is gentle but can be hot during the summer.

Alben W. Barkley (1877–1956)

Lake Barkley, created in 1966, is the third-largest lake in the state. It is named after Alben W. Barkley (left, standing next to President Truman), once the vice president of the United States. He was born in a log cabin near the town of Lowes. Barkley was one of the last political leaders who could claim a log-cabin birth. After working his way through college as a farmhand, he became a lawyer and served Kentucky in the U.S. Congress. As a senator during the Great Depression, he championed causes such as laws banning child labor. Barkley was vice president of the United States from 1949 to 1953 under President Harry Truman. He died just hours after delivering a speech to college students in which he declared, "[I] would rather be a servant in the house of the Lord than to sit in the seats of the mighty." ■

January temperature ranges from 23°F (–5°C) to 43°F (6°C); while the July temperature ranges from 66°F (19°C) to 87°F (31°C). The highest temperature ever recorded in Kentucky was 114°F (46°C) at Greensburg in July 1930. The lowest temperature on record was –34°F (–37°C) at Cynthiana in January 1963.

Caves, Kentucky's Special Treasure

Geologists who study the structure of the earth tell us that certain conditions must be met for the formation of underground caves. The first requirement is water. The second is large deposits of water-soluble rock such as limestone. As water seeps into limestone it dissolves the rock, creating openings or caves. The cave-making process is slow, taking hundreds of thousands of years. Kentucky meets these requirements, and as a result it has a wealth of caves.

A Tour of Mammoth Cave National Park

Mammoth Cave is one of the great wonders of North America. Every year almost 2 million tourists come to see this masterpiece of nature. It was made a national park in 1941. Situated about 30 miles (48 km) north of Bowling Green, the parklands spread over about 80 square miles (207 sq km). The grounds outside, laced with nature trails, are home to deer and wild turkeys.

Upon entering Mammoth Cave, visitors take guided tours through 12 miles (19 km) of trails open to the public. The guests choose among tours ranging from 1 to 4 miles (2 to 6 km) in length. Tour groups pass underground lakes, rivers, and even waterfalls.

The longest river, Echo River, is home to an unusual species of eyeless fish. The cave also has blind beetles and crayfish that have lived for millions of generations in the darkness.

Visitors gasp when they see phenomenal rock formations such as Frozen Niagara (which resembles a waterfall) and the Bottomless Pit (actually about 200 feet [61 m] deep). Tourist paths are well lit and suitable for walking.

The guides, who are National Park Service rangers, are experts on the cave's natural wonders and history. ■

One of the state's unofficial nicknames is "The Land of 10,000 Sinkholes."

Surveys show that Kentucky has about 765 miles (1,231 km) of caves that have been explored and mapped. No doubt, far more caverns below the surface have yet to be discovered. The granddaddy of all is Mammoth Cave. With 340 miles (547 km) of surveyed passages, Mammoth Cave is the world's longest cave system. Four other Kentucky caves are listed among the fifty longest caves in the world: the Fisher-Ridge cave system (48 miles [77 km] long) in Hart County; Sloans Valley Cave (25 miles [40 km] long) in Pulaski County; Whigpistle Cave (22.5 miles [36 km] long) in Edmonson County; and Hidden River Cave (19.5 miles [31 km] long) in Hart County.

Human presence in Mammoth Cave is a long story with an element of mystery. Settlers from the East entered the cave in the late 1700s. They found saltpeter, a key ingredient in making

Kentucky's state parks

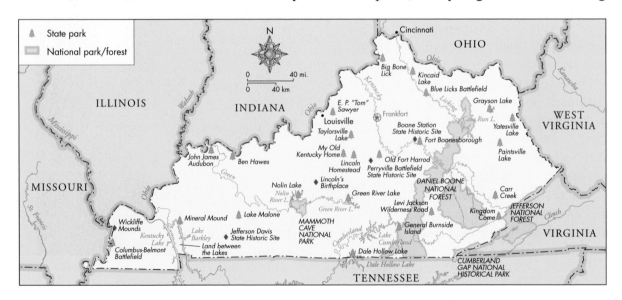

The Cavers

Cavers—cave explorers—enter a pitch-dark, damp, and jagged world. But it is a world full of surprises. Cavers delight in probing into caverns hoping for the thrill of discovery. No one knows when a bend in the rocks will open up into a broad chamber filled with fabulous crystal formations, never before seen by human eyes. Such discoveries are once-in-a-lifetime experiences. Mostly, cavers crawl, creep, and squirm through tortuous passageways they nickname Agony Avenue or Corkscrew Way. In 1972, a group of cavers discovered a link between Mammoth Cave and the Flint Ridge cave system. Many other spectacular discoveries still await cavers in Kentucky's amazing cave country. ■

gunpowder. Much of the gunpowder used in the War of 1812 came from saltpeter mined in the Mammoth Cave.

The cave became a tourist attraction in the early 1800s. At that time, its most famous tour guide was a slave named Stephen Bishop. In 1838, Bishop pushed a log ladder over the forbidding Bottomless Pit and crawled across. He then penetrated farther into the cave than anyone else of his era. Some 12 miles (19 km) into the cave, Bishop discovered an ancient skeleton. We now know that the skeleton is more than 2,000 years old. People of the Woodland period mined crystals from caves. The crystals may have had a religious significance. It is a mystery, however, why that person 2,000 years ago ventured so far into Mammoth Cave and died there.

The World of Nature

The pioneers found forests practically everywhere in Kentucky. Today, forests cover about half the state. Standing in the woodlands are oak, hickory, four species of magnolia, hemlock, pine, and the Kentucky coffee tree. In the spring, meadows are ablaze with mountain magnolias, rhododendrons, azaleas, and wild plums.

Of course the most famous plant associated with the state is bluegrass, the source of Kentucky's nickname. Actually it is dark green, not blue. For a couple of weeks in the spring its buds give out a bluish haze. Strangely, bluegrass is not native to the Bluegrass State. The grass came from England. It is believed its seed somehow got mixed with livestock feed and was brought across the Atlantic in the early 1600s. On North American soil, it spread

The Kentucky Coffee Tree

Found throughout the eastern United States, the Kentucky coffee tree grows as high as 100 feet (31 m). Often it stands alone on riverbank clearings. Early settlers brewed the seeds to make a coffeelike drink, hence the name. Until 1994 the Kentucky coffee tree was Kentucky's official state tree. ■

The Land between the Lakes

Situated between Lake Kentucky and Lake Barkley, the Land between the Lakes is a delightful area in which to explore Kentucky's world of nature. Extending into Tennessee, the Land between the Lakes covers 170,000 acres (68,850 ha). About 90 percent of the region is forestland. Some 200 miles (322 km) of hiking trails wind through these lovely woodlands. Birdwatchers are some of the most avid visitors. More than 250 species of birds have been observed in the Land between the Lakes. ■

quickly. When Daniel Boone first entered Kentucky, bluegrass was already common. Indians called it "white man's foot grass."

The world of nature has many faces in Kentucky's various regions. The Appalachian Plateau in the east has forested mountains and rushing rivers. The Bluegrass Region boasts gently rolling hills. Caves abound in the Mississippi Plateau. Wetlands are featured in the Jackson Purchase region. Rich farmland graces the Western Coal Fields area.

Wild animals in Kentucky include deer, foxes, mink, opossums, raccoons, and woodchucks. Rare and disappearing animals are the black bear, swamp rabbit, river otter, and cougar. Some 300 bird species make Kentucky their home, including Kentucky cardinals (the official state bird), herons, crows, wild ducks and geese, and woodpeckers. About 200 varieties of fish swim in Kentucky's rivers and lakes. Common fish are bluegills, crappies, muskellunge, rockfish, and walleyes. The state record rockfish, caught in Lake Cumberland in 1985, weighed 58 pounds (26 kg). But fish stories are common among anglers in this state, and some fishers say they've pulled in even bigger ones.

Deer are among the many animals that live in Kentucky's wilderness.

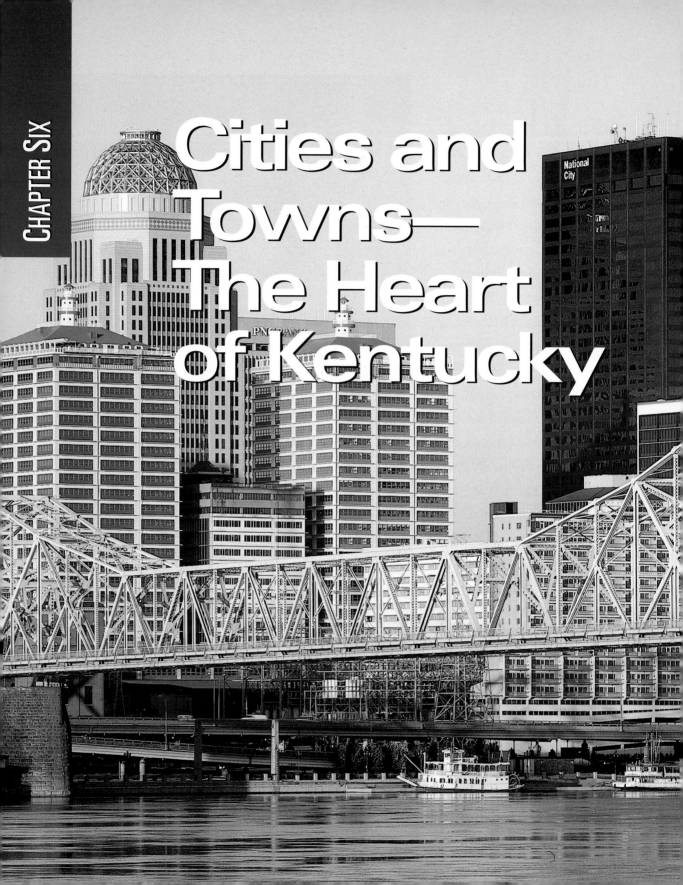

CHAPTER SIX

Cities and Towns—
The Heart
of Kentucky

Kentucky is a small-town state. Until recent years, most of its people lived in farming areas or in tiny villages. Even today, the state's largest city, Louisville, has only about 270,000 inhabitants. That population makes Louisville a midsized urban center by national standards. Small towns offer a comfortable way of life that Kentuckians refuse to abandon. Loyalty to one's town is expressed in cheering for the high school basketball team and in passionate efforts to keep streets clean and safe. Such loyalty is another example of the Kentuckians' love of home.

Morehead is a small college town.

The Towns of Eastern Kentucky

Eastern Kentucky is a mixed region. First, it is a tourist area, because of its wooded mountains and rushing rivers. Second, it is impoverished because workers have to contend with the boom-or-bust coal industry. Still, visitors fall in love with the eastern part of the State.

Ashland is the largest city in eastern Kentucky. Located on the banks of the Ohio River, it was settled in 1786, but it was a community long before that. Indians of the Woodland period once lived here. Burial grounds dating back to 800 B.C. are preserved in the city's downtown Central Park. Other Native American relics are on display at Ashland's Kentucky Highlands Museum.

To the south lies the eastern Kentucky town of Morehead. It thrived as a lumbering center until the trees ran out in the 1920s.

Opposite: The Louisville skyline

The Hatfields and the McCoys

Near the eastern Kentucky city of Pikeville lies the old McCoy farm, the scene of perhaps the most famous family feud in U.S. history. Legends say the clash began in 1878 when a pig wandered from the McCoy farm in Kentucky to the Hatfield farm in West Virginia. The McCoys accused the Hatfields of stealing the pig. A shooting war broke out between the two families that lasted ten years and cost a dozen lives. It was not the longest or even the bloodiest feud to rage between families in the Appalachians. But the Hatfield and McCoy conflict achieved fame because it was celebrated in folk songs and poetry. Songwriters delighted in the family names, which were musical and easy to rhyme. One song started with the lines:

Oh, the Hatfields and McCoys,
They were fearless mountain
boys. ■

Today, it is a quiet college town. Morehead State University was founded in 1922 as a tiny teachers' college. The university, with about 8,000 students, is now the focus of the town. While quiet in modern times, Morehead was the scene of a violent political feud that raged during Kentucky's period of strife. In 1884, an election held touched off a series of shootings known as the Rowan County War.

Prestonsburg is a city in transition. It was once a coal-mining center, and Prestonsburg's workers had to cope with long periods of joblessness when the price of coal went down. In recent years, tourism has bloomed in Prestonsberg. Guests come to see nearby attractions such as the Paintsville Lake State Park, the 672,000-acre (272,160 ha) Daniel Boone National Forest, and the Coal Camp Museum. Because of tourism, jobs have returned to Prestonsburg despite the ever-changing price of coal.

Spring in Daniel Boone National Forest

Central Kentucky

Drive the roads in the central part of the state and you see miles and miles of white or brown board fences. Prancing about inside the

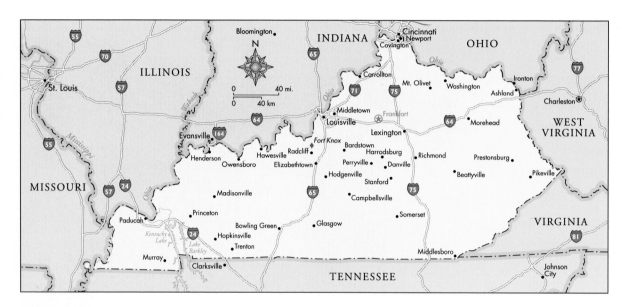

Kentucky's cities and interstates

fences are some of the most beautiful horses in the world. Central Kentucky is the heart of the Bluegrass Region. Hills here roll like waves on the sea, and fertile soil provides rich pastureland for horses. Yet central Kentucky is more than just bluegrass and horse country. It is the most populous and the most prosperous part of the state. The central region is also Kentucky's historic soul, the land of the pioneers.

Lexington, Kentucky's second-largest city, is the home of the University of Kentucky, where some 23,000 students attend classes. The university helps to make Lexington the state's cultural capital. Lexington has the University of Kentucky Art Museum, the William S. Webb Museum of Anthropology, the Kentucky Gallery of Fine Arts and Crafts, and the Lexington Children's Museum. Many visitors take a delightful tour of the city's historic houses.

The Kentucky Horse Park

The first Thoroughbred horse was brought to Lexington in 1779, a full thirteen years before Kentucky became a state. Thus central Kentucky's love affair with fine horses is older than the state itself. You can learn about the state and its horses at the Kentucky Horse Park, near Lexington. A visit to the 1,032-acre (418 ha) park begins with a film about Kentucky racehorses called *Thou Shalt Fly without Wings*. Then guests take a farm tour to see more than forty breeds of horses and a harness maker at work. Bring a camera and take plenty of shots of horses. ■

Daniel Boone is buried in the Frankfort Cemetery.

Ashland was Henry Clay's home from 1811 until his death in 1852. The Mary Todd Lincoln House was the girlhood home of that First Lady.

Frankfort, the capital of Kentucky, lies in a lovely forest setting. It is a small city, the eighth in size within the state. Its skyline is dominated by the Kentucky state capitol, completed in 1910. The building is a splendid example of Greek architecture blended with ornate French styles. The old state capitol, erected in 1830, is now the Kentucky History Museum. The museum displays paintings of Kentucky heroes such as Henry Clay, Daniel Boone, and Madeline Breckinridge. In Frankfort Cemetery, a monument marks the grave of Daniel Boone, who died in 1820.

Historic towns and sites abound in the Lexington–Frankfort region. At Harrodsburg stands a recreation of Fort Harrod, the first successful pioneer settlement in the state. In 1792, Kentucky's first constitution was adopted in Danville's Constitution Square. Visitors to the square today see a restored pioneer church, jail, and log courthouse. A highlight of downtown Lexington is the Pleasant Green Missionary Baptist Church, the oldest African-American church west of the Appalachians. The church was founded in 1790 by a Virginia slave whose freedom was purchased by church members.

Richmond is the home of Eastern Kentucky University. Steeped in history, the town was the site of an 1862 Civil War battle that involved more than 50,000 soldiers. At Richmond's White Hall State Historic Site stands a restored forty-four-room mansion once owned by Kentucky's abolitionist leader Cassius M. Clay. Another resident of Richmond was Henry Allen Laine, an African-American poet who composed his works in the early 1900s, a time when few southern blacks ventured into poetry.

Sprawling along the Ohio River to the north is Louisville, Kentucky's largest city. One of its main attractions is the University of Louisville, a highly respected college, which also has powerful basketball teams. Louisville is one of the few cities its size that has its own symphony orchestra as well as a nationally known theater company—the Actor's Theater of Louisville. Louisville also has the J. B. Speed Art Museum, the Kentucky Derby Museum, the Louisville Zoo, and the Kentucky Kingdom Amusement Park.

A Famous Resident of Louisville

In 1784, fourteen-year-old William Clark and his family moved to what was then the muddy village of Louisville. One of Louisville's founders was General George Rogers Clark, a Revolutionary War hero. William Clark was the general's younger brother. As a teenager, William Clark learned how to navigate flatboats on the Ohio River. That knowledge served him very well in 1803 when President Thomas Jefferson chose him as co-leader of the Lewis and Clark expedition. That daring journey blazed a trail over the unexplored lands of the West. ■

Fort Knox

The sprawling military base of Fort Knox is near Louisville. The base covers 109,000 acres (44,145 ha). Here, the U.S. Army developed tank and infantry tactics in the years before World War II. Also on the base is the Patton Museum of Cavalry and Armor. The museum displays armored fighting vehicles and the personal effects of World War II commander General George Patton. However, the best-known feature of Fort Knox is the billions of dollars of gold stored in its vaults. This fabulous treasure makes up the U.S. gold reserve, which backs the value of the dollar. Over the years, movies and stories have been written about outlaws who break into Fort Knox to steal the gold. Such grand theft operations do not happen, and any thief would be foolish to try. The vaults at Fort Knox are among the most heavily guarded places in the nation. ■

Western Kentucky

West along the Ohio River lies Owensboro, the state's third-largest city. Owensboro claims to be a party town, a place of fine food and bluegrass music. During Owensboro's annual International Bar-B-Q Festival more than 20 tons of barbecued delicacies are served to guests. On the slightly more serious side, the Owensboro Museum of Fine Arts displays works by some of Kentucky's best painters.

Near Owensboro is the historic river town of Hawesville. A young Abraham Lincoln was once taken to court in Hawesville, charged with operating a riverboat without a license. The eighteen-year-old future president argued his case so well that the Hawesville judge urged him to study law. The rest—as we know—is history.

Paducah's past is so rich that it has more historic markers than any other Kentucky city. It was founded in 1827 by William Clark of Lewis and Clark fame. The city's history is depicted in *Paducah—Wall to Wall*, a huge series of murals painted on a downtown

Paducah was founded by William Clark in 1827.

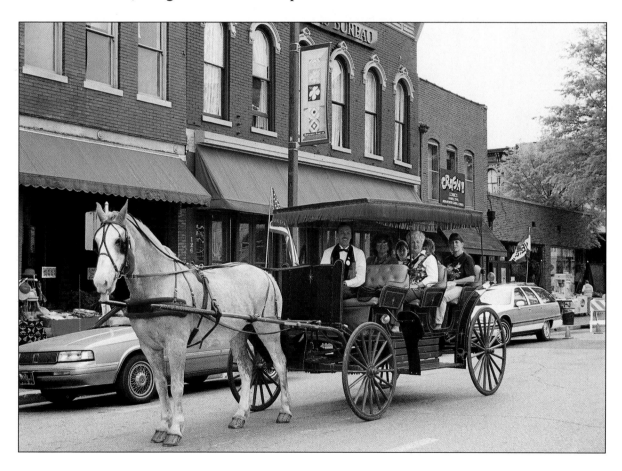

The William Floyd Collins Saga

William Floyd Collins was born in 1887 on a tiny farm at Flint Ridge, just a few miles from Mammoth Cave. He spent much of his youth crawling around caves in western Kentucky. While exploring Sand Cave in 1925, he dislodged a rock and caught his leg. A rescue squad was able to locate Collins and talk to him but could not pull him from the cave. For more than two weeks, a crew worked frantically to dig a tunnel to the trapped man. Newspapers reported the effort. Huge crowds came to Sand Cave but served only to hamper the rescuers. When the tunnel-diggers finally reached Collins, he was dead. A popular outdoor play, *The Floyd Collins Story*, is put on every summer in Brownsville dramatizing the tragedy. ■

wall. One of the events depicted on the mural is the 1937 flood that inundated 90 percent of the town.

Kentuckians call the highway running west of Paducah the Great River Road. Along the Ohio River, the road passes through Barlow. Some 200 years of Barlow's history are on display at the Barlow House Museum. Below Barlow is the point where the Ohio River merges with the Mississippi River. Further along the Great River Road is Henderson, which the writer Mark Twain once hailed as "the most beautiful town on the Mississippi."

Well south of the Ohio River in western Kentucky is the city of Bowling Green, founded in 1798. Some historians believe its name honored the established city of Bowling Green, Virginia. Other scholars say the town was named after an early resident who ran a sort of outside bowling alley where people played a game called "bowling on the green." The opening of auto plants has contributed to Bowling Green's growth in recent years. Bowling Green is home to Western Kentucky University.

The region outside Bowling Green is cave country. Nearby Mammoth Cave is the major attraction, but dozens of other caves and caverns also lure tourists. Visitors to Park City are thrilled by Diamond Caverns with its thousands of stalactites and colorful flowstone. Crystal Onyx Cave in Cave City features fascinating crystalline formations. The town of Horse Cave is home to the American Cave Museum and Hidden River Cave.

CHAPTER SEVEN

Kentucky
Government

entucky is officially called a "commonwealth." The name dates back to the 1780s when the western lands that became Kentucky were owned by the Commonwealth of Virginia. Three other states—Massachusetts, Pennsylvania, and Virginia—are also officially called commonwealths. The word *commonwealth* means "for the good of all." Apart from the name, Kentucky's commonwealth status is of little real importance. In all respects, the Commonwealth of Kentucky functions as a typical state within the U.S. family of states.

The Jefferson Davis Salute to Kentucky

The Government at Work

Kentucky is governed by its constitution, which was written in 1891. Previous constitutions were adopted in 1792, 1799, and 1850. The present constitution has been amended, or changed, many times over the last 100 years. All amendments must be approved by the majority of voters in a general election.

The constitution divides the state government into three branches or departments: the executive branch, the legislative branch, and the judicial branch. The executive department is pledged to carry out laws. The legislative branch creates new laws and rescinds old ones. The judicial department tries legal cases and interprets the constitution.

Opposite: The State Capitol in Frankfort

Kentucky's State Government

Executive Branch

```
                         ┌─────────────┐
                         │  Governor   │
                         └─────────────┘
```

Lieutenant Governor	Secretary of State	Attorney General	State Treasurer	Auditor of Public Accounts	Commissioner of Agriculture	Superintendent of Public Instruction

Legislative Branch

```
              ┌──────────────────┐
              │ General Assembly  │
              └──────────────────┘
```

Senate	House of Representatives

Judicial Branch

Supreme Court
Court of Appeals
Circuit Courts
Municipal Courts

Dividing government into three branches is called the system of checks and balances or the division of powers. In theory, no one branch can assume dictatorial powers because it is kept in check by the other branches. The federal government of the United States is also structured into three departments.

The executive department is headed by the governor, who is elected to a four-year term. He or she has the power to call out the state militia in cases of emergency. Other officers in

Kentucky's Governors

Name	Party	Term	Name	Party	Term
Isaac Shelby	Dem.-Rep.*	1792–1796	William O. Bradley	Rep.	1895–1899
James Garrard	Dem.-Rep.*	1796–1804	William S. Taylor	Rep.	1899–1900
Christopher Greenup	Dem.-Rep.*	1804–1808	William Goebel	Dem.	1900
Charles Scott	Dem.-Rep.*	1808–1812	J. C. W. Beckham	Dem.	1900–1907
Isaac Shelby	Dem.-Rep.*	1812–1816	Augustus E. Willson	Rep.	1907–1911
George Madison	Dem.-Rep.*	1816–1819	James B. McCreary	Dem.	1911–1915
Gabriel Slaughter	Dem.-Rep.*	1819–1820	Augustus O. Stanley	Dem.	1915–1919
John Adair	Dem.-Rep.*	1820–1824	James D. Black	Dem.	1919
Joseph Desha	Dem.-Rep.*	1824–1828	Edwin P. Morrow	Rep.	1919–1923
Thomas Metcalfe	Nat. Rep.†	1828–1832	William J. Fields	Dem.	1923–1927
John Breathitt	Dem.	1832–1834	Flem D. Sampson	Rep.	1927–1931
James T. Morehead	Nat. Rep.†	1834–1836	Ruby Laffoon	Dem.	1931–1935
James Clark	Whig	1836–1839	Albert B. Chandler	Dem.	1935–1939
Charles A. Wickliffe	Whig	1839–1840	Keen Johnson	Dem.	1939–1943
Robert P. Letcher	Whig	1840–1844	Simeon S. Willis	Rep.	1943–1947
William Owsley	Whig	1844–1848	Earle C. Clements	Dem.	1947–1950
John J. Crittenden	Whig	1848–1850	Lawrence W. Wetherby	Dem.	1950–1955
John L. Helm	Whig	1850–1851			
Lazarus W. Powell	Dem.	1851–1855	Albert B. Chandler	Dem.	1955–1959
Charles S. Morehead	Know-Nothing	1855–1859	Bert T. Combs	Dem.	1959–1963
			Edward T. Breathitt	Dem.	1963–1967
Beriah Magoffin	Dem.	1859-1862	Louie B. Nunn	Rep.	1967–1971
James F. Robinson	Union	1862-1863	Wendell Ford	Dem.	1971–1974
Thomas E. Bramlette	Union	1863–1867	Julian M. Carroll	Dem.	1974–1979
John L. Helm	Dem.	1867	John Y. Brown, Jr.	Dem.	1979–1983
John W. Stevenson	Dem.	1867–1871	Martha Layne Collins	Dem.	1983–1987
Preston H. Leslie	Dem.	1871–1875	Wallace G. Wilkinson	Dem.	1987–1991
James B. McCreary	Dem.	1875–1879	Brereton C. Jones	Dem.	1991–1995
Luke P. Blackburn	Dem.	1879–1883	Paul E. Patton	Dem.	1995–
J. Proctor Knott	Dem.	1883–1887			
Simon B. Buckner	Dem.	1887–1891	*Democratic-Republican		
John Young Brown	Dem.	1891–1895	†National Republican		

The State Flag

Kentucky's official state flag has a blue field with a picture of the state seal and the words of the state motto in the middle.

The state seal, which dates back to 1792, shows a pioneer and a diplomat greeting each other with a warm embrace.

The state motto, "United We Stand, Divided We Fall," comes from a ballad called the "Liberty Song," which was popular during the Revolutionary War. The design of the state flag was approved by state government in 1928. The original flag is now displayed in the Kentucky History Museum in Frankfort. ■

Kentucky's State Symbols

State nickname: The Bluegrass State More than 200 years ago, travelers noticed that the buds of central Kentucky grasses cast a bluish haze in the spring. They began to ask where they could get seeds for this pretty "bluegrass of Kentucky." The term endured as the state nickname.

State flower: Goldenrod The name "golden" fits this common flower, which blooms in the summer and fall and covers the ground with its bright yellow blooms. The plant is found throughout Kentucky. More than 100 species of goldenrod grow in North America and at least 30 of them are found in Kentucky.

State tree: Tulip tree This is sometimes wrongly called the tulip–poplar. It is not a poplar at all, but a member of the magnolia family. A stately tree, it can live for 200 years and grow to a height of 150 feet (45 m).

State bird: Kentucky cardinal With its cheerful song and colorful plumage, this bird has long delighted Kentuckians. The bright red males are often called *redbirds.*

State bluegrass song: "Blue Moon of Kentucky" Because Kentucky is so identified with bluegrass music, it is no wonder it has an official bluegrass song. "Blue Moon of Kentucky" is a lively number written in the 1940s by Bill Monroe, one of the founders of the bluegrass style.

State horse: Thoroughbred Certainly no other breed of horse could be as honored as Kentucky's state horse. Thoroughbred horses are derived

from Arabian ancestors. Excitable and spirited, they make the best racehorses. Over the years, Thoroughbreds raised in Kentucky have proved to be some of the swiftest in the world.

State fish: Kentucky bass Given their wealth of rivers and lakes, Kentuckians have always loved fishing. One of their prize catches is the bass, especially a species dubbed the Kentucky bass.

State butterfly: Viceroy Adopted in 1990 to support awareness for butterfly conservation, the viceroy butterfly (right) looks like another species of butterfly, the monarch. Found throughout Kentucky, monarchs are poisonous to birds which will not try to eat viceroys because of the resemblance.

State fossil: Brachiopod This fossil is common in most areas of Kentucky, so it was the perfect choice when students in one Louisville classroom decided on nominations for the state fossil. Among the oldest of fossils, brachiopods are mol-

lusks and have two valves, or shells.

State wild animal: Gray squirrel Common in both rural and urban areas, gray squirrels are the widest-known wild animal species in Kentucky. It was adopted partly because of its ability to cohabitate with people.

State gemstone: Freshwater pearl Kentuckians are proud of this cherished gem, found in lakes across the western part of the state. Harvested from mussels, freshwater pearls ornament the crown jewels of many countries' heads of state. ▪

Thou Shalt Not Duel

A duel—a ritualistic fight with pistols or swords—was once considered an honorable way for gentlemen to settle arguments. Bloody duels took so many lives in Kentucky that in 1849 a law was introduced prohibiting men who had fought duels from holding state office. To this day, the governor of Kentucky must swear he or she has never fought a duel. No other state has such an anti-dueling provision written into the governor's oath of office. ■

the executive department, also elected to four-year terms, are the lieutenant governor, the secretary of state, the attorney general, the state treasurer, the auditor of public accounts, the commissioner of agriculture, and the superintendent of public instruction.

The legislative branch is called the General Assembly. The General Assembly has two houses: the senate with 38 members,

Kentucky's senate chamber

Kentucky's State Song

"My Old Kentucky Home"

Written by Stephen Foster, the song became popular in the early 1850s. It was chosen as the state song in 1928. "My Old Kentucky Home" is played before the Kentucky Derby race, and it is played by just about every high school band in the state.

*The sun shines bright in the old
   Kentucky home
'tis summer, the people are gay,
the corn top's ripe and the
   meadow's in the bloom
while the birds make music all
   the day.
The young folks roll on the little
   cabin floor
all merry, all happy, and bright.
By'n by hard times comes a-
   knocking at the door,
then my old Kentucky home,
   good night.*

Chorus:
*Weep no more, my lady,
oh weep no more today.
We will sing one song for the
   old Kentucky home,
for the old Kentucky home far
   away.*

*They hunt no more for the
   'possum and the coon
on meadow, the hill and the
   shore.*

*They sing no more by the
   glimmer of the moon
on the bench by that old cabin
   door.
The day goes by like a shadow
   o'er the heart
with sorrow where all was
   delight.
The time has come when the
   people have to part
then my old Kentucky home,
   good night.*

*The head must bow and the
   back will have to bend
wherever the people may go.
A few more days and the trouble
   all will end
in the field where sugar-canes
   may grow.
A few more days for to tote the
   weary load.
No matter, 'twill never be light.
A few more days till we totter on
   the road,
then my old Kentucky home,
   good night.* ■

How a Bill Becomes a Law

Suppose the people of Todd County in southwestern Kentucky decide they need to build a new high school. The people then begin a long process. First, they apply for state funds to finance the project. Todd County men and women must inform their state legislators (their senators and representatives) of their needs. The legislators will then introduce a measure (called a bill) to the General Assembly. If the General Assembly approves Todd County's school-building bill, it next goes to the governor. When the governor signs the bill, it becomes state law.

However, the governor might decide that the school is not needed or is too costly. The governor will then veto, or refuse to sign, the bill. In the case of a veto, the bill is returned to the General Assembly. If a majority of both the senate and the house vote for the bill, it becomes a law in spite of the governor's veto. This process between the legislature and the governor must take place before the people of Todd County get state money to build their new high school. ■

and the house of representatives with 100 members. Senators are elected to four-year terms and members of the house are elected to two-year terms. Measures regarding taxing and spending are always chief concerns of the legislative branch.

Kentucky's counties

Kentucky's judicial branch is composed of four levels of courts: the supreme court, the court of appeals, circuit courts, and district courts. The supreme court is the highest court in the state. The supreme court reviews all judgments of lesser courts that impose sentences of death or more than twenty years imprisonment on defendants. The court system also has the important job of making sure no new state law violates the Kentucky Constitution.

Local government is administered by counties and towns. Kentucky has 120 counties, the third-largest number of counties in the nation (Texas has 254 and Georgia has 159). The local governments provide services such as the maintenance of roads, schools, and police forces.

Taxing and Spending

Everyone agrees that people need services such as excellent schools, well-maintained roads, and an effective police force. These services are usually provided by the government. And they cost money. The government raises money through taxes. Everyone also agrees they pay too much in taxes. This is the

Kentucky's taxes help support schools and maintain roads.

dilemma state government faces: how does Kentucky provide services and still not infuriate the people with higher taxes?

In the 1990s, Kentucky typically spent about $12 billion each year on state services. The state university system alone costs almost $2 billion annually. Expenses for grade schools and high schools near $3 billion. Add roads, jails, state-supported hospitals, salaries for state office workers, and hundreds of other costs, and the yearly budget reaches a staggering figure.

The Kentucky state lottery was started to raise money without raising taxes.

Where does the state get the money to fund such expensive programs? About 30 percent of the state's revenue comes from the federal government through programs such as federal aid to education. Another 30 percent comes from sales tax and individual income taxes paid by Kentuckians. The state collects a 6 percent sales tax on items bought in stores (food, medicine, and some other items are exempt from the sales tax). Income taxes are deducted from the paychecks of Kentucky workers. Corporations pay a separate tax. Revenue also comes from gasoline taxes and licenses. Local governments tax home owners according to the value of their homes.

Many states, including Kentucky, have turned to lotteries as a means of providing revenue without raising taxes. Kentucky's state lottery began operation in 1989. Ini-

James "Honest Dick" Tate

Kentucky has had many noble political leaders, but it has also had a few outright crooks. The most notorious scoundrel in the state's history was James Tate, who served as state treasurer. In 1888, Tate walked out of his office carrying two bags of gold and silver coins worth almost a quarter of a million dollars. All of this loot was tax money that had been collected from workers. After the theft, rumors said that Tate was living in luxury in China, Canada, and Brazil. He was never apprehended for his crime. The Tate incident made generations of Kentuckians distrust their elected officials. Tate, whose nickname was Dick, often campaigned under a bold banner: VOTE FOR "HONEST DICK" TATE. ■

tially, money collected by the lottery was intended for schools, for programs designed to aid the elderly, and to help veterans of the Vietnam War. Today, the state has allocated lottery funds for a wider range of uses. In recent years, the lottery has been criticized because it tempts poor people to spend their money on get-rich-quick dreams instead of on food and other necessities.

CHAPTER EIGHT

The Economy at Work

Years ago, Kentucky was known for producing coal, racehorses, whiskey, tobacco, farm products, and little else. Few major factories operated in the state. Happily, the economic picture has changed. Today, Kentucky ranks twentieth among the fifty states in the value of manufactured goods it produces. State factories turn out products worth more than $50 billion each year. Many pockets of poverty remain in Kentucky, but in the 1990s the state has made great strides in creating jobs for the people.

Steel mills are among the many industries that make up Kentucky's economy.

Industries

Kentucky has more than 4,400 manufacturing plants. These factories produce cars, trucks, clothing, industrial chemicals, and machinery. Manufacturing accounts for almost 20 percent of the state's jobs.

Transportation equipment is the leading product manufactured within the state. The huge Toyota plant in Georgetown now builds 400,000 Camry and Avalon cars annually. Bowling Green is another large car-manufacturing center. Other transportation equipment made in the state includes trucks, airplane parts, trailers of

Opposite: A Kentucky farmer in his tobacco field

various kinds, and railroad cars. In all, some 36,000 Kentuckians hold jobs making transportation equipment.

Chemical products rank second within the state. Factories in the Louisville area manufacture paint. Plants in Carrollton make silicones and chemical coatings. Other chemical plants operate in Ashland, Owensboro, Elizabethtown, Calvert City, Paducah, and Brandenberg. The manufacture of machines and machinery parts is Kentucky's third-ranking industry. Pulleys and ball bearings are made in Maysville. Heating and air-conditioning equipment and farm machines are assembled in Louisville. Also in Louisville are factories making plumbing fixtures and air-pollution–control equipment.

Food–processing has long been an important Kentucky industry. In the 1990s, food and food products were a $5.2 billion-per-year business. And Kentucky leads the nation in whiskey production. Whiskey is not a food, but it is distilled from corn and grain. The Bluegrass State makes almost half the nation's whiskey. Other Kentucky plants make soft drinks and meat products. A large plant in Mayfield produces packaged baked goods.

Heaven Hill

Guests are invited to visit a giant whiskey-making facility near Bardstown called Heaven Hill. It is the world's second-largest producer of bourbon whiskey.

Bourbon is a special blend of whiskey developed in Kentucky more than 200 years ago. Some people call bourbon made in the Bluegrass State "Kentucky sippin' whiskey." Visitors at Heaven Hill pass barrels where more than 25 million gallons (94.6 million l) of bourbon are aging.

Laws forbid guests at Heaven Hill from tasting the product. In fact, though Kentucky is the nation's leading whiskey maker, more than half of its 120 counties are "dry," meaning the sale of alcohol is forbidden within the county's boundaries. Kentucky authorities acknowledge that whiskey is a dangerous drink in the wrong hands. ■

Agriculture and Mining

In the mid-1990s, Kentucky had about 91,000 farms. The state's average-size farm was 155 acres (63 ha). This is small by national standards. The Kentucky tradition of maintaining small, family-owned farms goes against a nationwide trend to develop farming enterprises on huge tracts of land. Kentucky farms produce more than $3 billion in goods and rank about twentieth in the nation in overall agricultural production.

Tobacco remains the state's most valuable crop. Kentucky is second only to North Carolina as a tobacco producer. Tobacco was first raised in Kentucky in the 1780s. Other crops include corn, hay, soybeans, barley, and oats. Apples are grown on farms near the towns of Liberty and Walton. Popcorn is a favorite crop in Calloway County. Livestock accounts for more than half of Kentucky's total farm income. The same grasses that nurture champion racehorses feed cattle and dairy cows. Hogs and chickens are grown throughout the state.

Farming continues to be important to Kentucky.

Bibb Lettuce, a Kentucky First

John Bibb was a respected lawyer in Frankfort during the 1820s and 1830s. He was also an amateur horticulturalist. Bibb developed a variety of lettuce that was resis- tant to lice. His dark-leaved plant grew in small loose clusters. Bibb called his invention "limestone lettuce." It later became the very popular Bibb lettuce. ■

Although the small farm remains the backbone of Kentucky agriculture, the farm population across the state is decreasing. Today, only 2 percent of the state's workers hold farm jobs. The current figure of 91,000 farms is down from 133,000 farms in 1964. Yet Kentucky's farm production per acre is much higher than it was three decades ago. Better equipment and fertilizers have made the state's farms more efficient.

Kentucky's natural resources

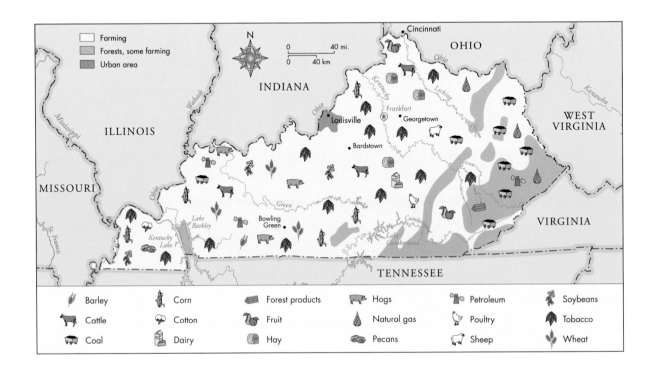

Coal is still Kentucky's most important mineral product. In the 1990s, Kentucky's coal production ranked among the top three of the fifty states. Coal is mined both in the eastern Kentucky mountains and in the Western Coal Fields region. Additional minerals include crushed stone, natural gas, and petroleum.

Other Industries

More Kentuckians work in service industries than in any other field. A service worker does not create a product. Instead he or she provides a service for customers. Bank clerks, waiters and waitresses, and schoolteachers are service workers. Tourism is the state's biggest source of service jobs. About 9,000 businesses—such as hotels and restaurants—are devoted to serving out-of-state visitors. Every year, tourists contribute more than $7 billion to the state's economy. Some 145,000 people are employed in tourist-related businesses.

Kentucky has more than 2,900 miles (4,666 km) of railroad track. Passenger service, once important, has dwindled to just a few

These coal workers mine Kentucky's most important mineral product.

Most of Kentucky's railroads are used for transporting coal.

Some Random and Unusual Facts about Kentucky's Economy

Barren County has the state's most fertile farmland.

Bourbon County is dry—no bourbon or any other alcohol is sold there.

All the Corvettes made by the Chevrolet Auto Company are manufactured in Bowling Green.

Kaelin's Restaurant in Louisville claims to have served the nation's first cheeseburger in 1934.

Machines in a Louisville tobacco-processing plant churn out 5,000 cigarettes an hour.

Surveys report that the people of Pikeville, Kentucky, drink more Pepsi-Cola per person than the people of any other city in the United States.

In 1829, workers at Burkesville were drilling a water well when they struck oil. The oil gushed 50 feet (15 m) in the air. The workers had accidentally created the world's first free-flowing oil well. ■

travelers. About 90 percent of railway tonnage originating in Kentucky is made up of coal shipments. Approximately 73,000 miles (117,457 km) of federal, state, and local roads connect all of the state's cities and towns. Five major airports service scheduled airline travelers. The five airports are located at Lexington, Louisville, Owensboro, Paducah, and Erlanger. The city of Erlanger, near the

What Kentucky Grows, Manufactures, and Mines

Agriculture	Manufacturing	Mining
Tobacco	Transportation equipment	Coal
Beef cattle	Chemicals	
Horses	Machinery	
Milk	Food products	
Corn		
Soybeans		

Ohio River, has a large airport used by passengers bound for Covington, Kentucky, and Cincinnati, Ohio.

The state has twenty-six daily newspapers. The *Louisville Courier-Journal* enjoys the largest circulation, and the *Lexington Herald-Leader* is next largest. In the mid-1990s, the state had 296 radio stations, 20 commercial television stations, and 16 public television stations.

CHAPTER NINE

A Look at the Kentuckians

A 1939 book called *Kentucky—A Guide to the Bluegrass State* said, "Wherever a Kentuckian may be, he is more than willing to boast of the beauties and virtues of his native state. He believes without reservation that Kentucky is the garden spot of the world,

Kentucky is home to many kinds of people.

and is ready to dispute with anyone who questions the claim." Though the book was written decades ago, the pride Kentuckians feel for their state remains true to this day. People born in Kentucky pour forth their love of the Bluegrass State no matter where they live now.

Population Trends

A century ago, most Kentuckians—and most U.S. residents—lived in farming communities. But across the country there was a steady tendency for people to move from rural areas to the cities. By 1920, more than 50 percent of U.S. residents were city dwellers. Not so in Kentucky. It was not until the 1970 census when Kentucky's city dwellers outnumbered its rural residents. Even in 1990, Kentucky's urban population was only 52 percent, far below the national average of 75.2 percent.

Louisville and Lexington have the largest concentrations of people. Covington, which also serves as a suburb of Cincinnati, Ohio, is another thickly populated area. Other major urban

Opposite: Enjoying a day at Churchill Downs

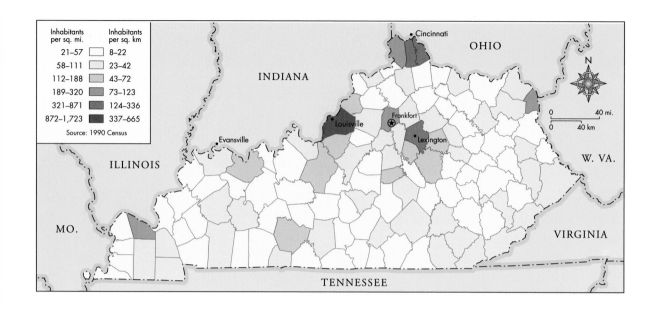

Kentucky's population density

Population of Kentucky's Major Cities (1990)

Louisville	269,063
Lexington	225,366
Owensboro	53,549
Covington	43,264
Bowling Green	40,641
Hopkinsville	29,809

centers are Bowling Green, Owensboro, and Paducah. By contrast, many areas of southern and eastern Kentucky are scarcely populated.

In 1990, Kentucky had 3,698,969 people, ranking twenty-third in population among the fifty states. The state's 1990 population represented a growth of only 1 percent since 1980, while the U.S. population gain was 9.8 percent. Louisville, the state's largest city, lost population between 1980 and 1990. Despite the improving economy of recent years, many Kentucky families still move elsewhere to find better-paying jobs. Consequently Kentucky's population growth lags behind most other states'.

Who Are the Kentuckians?

There are no "typical" Kentuckians. Many eastern Kentuckians have lived for generations in rural isolation and therefore differ radically from people who live in Lexington. Ways of life vary between city dwellers and those on farms. But some generalizations can be made to describe the people of the Bluegrass State.

Kentucky is not as ethnically diverse as the more industrial states in the East and the Midwest. The population is 92 percent white according to the 1990 census. Some 7 percent of Kentuckians are African-American. Persons of Hispanic descent make up 0.6 percent of the population; Asians, 0.5 percent; and American Indians, 0.2 percent. Immigrants are less than 1 percent of the total population. Only a small number of Kentucky families speak a language other than English at home.

Economic figures reveal that Kentuckians make less money than most other U.S. residents. In 1995, Kentucky ranked forty-third among the fifty states in per capita

African-Americans make up 7 percent of Kentucky's population.

Speaking Kentuckian

Kentuckians speak proper English; it's the other people in the country that have accents. At least that's what a Kentuckian will tell you. Certain Kentucky speech patterns stand apart from the general southern drawl heard in the state. Kids in central Kentucky don't play on seesaws, they play on "ridyhorses." Some Kentuckians call a moth a "candlefly," and others call earthworms "redworms." Also, a young man does not take his date to the movies or to a dance, he "carries" her there. In eastern Kentucky, older people still say "writ" for wrote and "clumb" for climbed. But remember, they don't have an accent—outsiders do. ■

(per person) earnings. Of the other border states, only West Virginia lagged behind Kentucky in per capita income. Within the state, Kentuckians in city areas earned up to 20 percent more than did rural dwellers. Studies show, however, that the cost of living in Kentucky is slightly lower than in the nation as a whole.

Kentucky is Bible Belt country, where people take religion seriously. Especially in rural Kentucky, the church is the foundation of a community. The state is overwhelmingly Protestant. Almost 1 million Kentuckians are Southern Baptists. Roman Catholics total about 365,000 people, and there are some 14,800 Jews.

Religion is an important part of life in Kentucky.

Schools

Kentucky law declares that all children from age six through sixteen must attend school. Public schools are the rule in the state. In the mid-1990s, some 634,100 pupils attended public elementary

The Shakers of Old Kentucky

Almost 200 years ago, groups of Shakers settled in South Union near Bowling Green and in Pleasant Hill near Harrodsburg. The Shakers believed that they could come into direct contact with God through passionate prayer. So intense were their prayer sessions that people quivered and shook, giving rise to the sect's name. The Shaker communities began to fade in the mid-1800s. Visitors today tour the Historic Shaker Village of Pleasant Hill where they eat authentic Shaker recipes and marvel at the furniture built long ago by this devoted religious group. ■

Most students in Kentucky attend public schools.

and high schools, while only about 66,000 went to private and parochial schools.

Kentucky employs more than 37,000 classroom teachers. Kentucky was the first state in the nation to bring its school system into the Internet age. All of its 176 school districts are currently online.

The University of Louisville

This allows students to use the Internet to find information when writing reports.

More than 175,000 college students attend classes in Kentucky today. The state has thirty-six degree-granting universities and colleges. The largest state-supported colleges are the Univer-

Kentucky Schools, a Historic Commitment

Even in the days when most Kentuckians lived near forts and feared Indian attacks, schools and classrooms operated in Kentucky. The state's first school dates to 1775 at Fort Harrod.

The fort's teacher, Mrs. William Coomes, had her students write with charcoal pencils on slates made of tree bark. Children also attended one-room log-cabin schools in the outposts of Boonesborough and Logan's Station.

Instead of cash, the teachers were paid with rations of corn, beef jerky, and beer. Many frontier teachers knew only a little more about reading and writing than their pupils. ■

Berea College, a Unique Institution

Berea College, in the town of Berea, was founded in 1866. From its beginnings, blacks and whites and men and women attended classes on an equal basis. It was one of the first southern schools to be integrated. Berea College is tuition-free. The college requires each of its 1,500 students to work ten to fifteen hours a week on campus projects to offset costs.

sity of Kentucky at Lexington, the University of Louisville at Louisville, Eastern Kentucky University at Richmond, and Western Kentucky University at Bowling Green. Kentucky Wesleyan in Owensboro is a major private college and is famous for its excellence in athletics. The state's oldest college is Transylvania University in Lexington. Founded in 1780, Transylvania University was named after an early land-developing enterprise called the Transylvania Company.

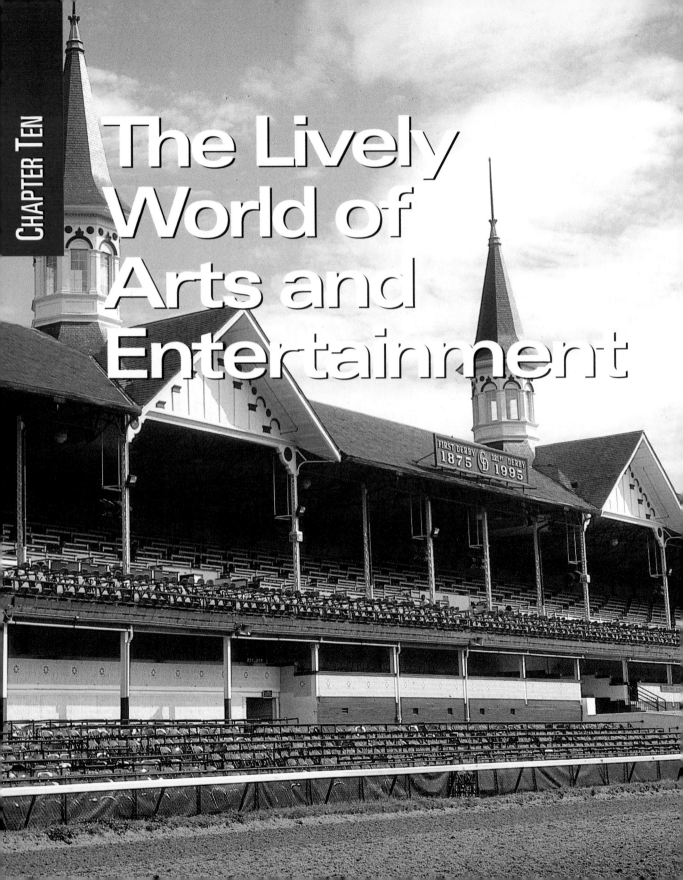

CHAPTER TEN

The Lively World of Arts and Entertainment

FIRST DERBY 1875 CD 121st DERBY 1995

Theres the toe-tapping beat of bluegrass music. There's the thrill of horses bursting out of the starting gate. And there are the marvels of folk art and crafts. All this—and friendly people too—contribute to Kentucky's unique charm.

Sports

Fierce pride their home state is a common feeling among Kentuckians. In few other arenas is that pride expressed more fervently than in college basketball. The University of Louisville, the University of Kentucky, and Kentucky Wesleyan dominate sports pages in newspapers throughout the state. Old men sit in restaurants retelling the stories of dramatic games played years ago. Kids shoot and dribble on schoolyard courts hoping to play like college stars.

Women's basketball is also popular in Kentucky. High school basketball for boys and girls fills stadiums, especially in the small towns. But men's college basketball is an epic game in the Bluegrass State. Coaches such as Adolph Rupp, Clem Haskins, and Rick Pitino are legends. Players of the past—Wes Unseld (Louisville), Dan Issel (University of Kentucky), and Antoine Walker (University of Kentucky)—are hailed as heroes. This incredible fan loyalty has translated into success. Season after season, Kentucky college teams challenge for championships. In 1996 and 1998, the University of Kentucky Wildcats continued their glorious tradition by winning the NCAA men's basketball championship. The Wildcats have captured seven titles in the school's history.

Wesley Unseld played for the University of Louisville in the 1960s.

Opposite: Churchill Downs

Adolph Rupp, Controversial Coach

Adolph Rupp coached the University of Kentucky Wildcats from 1930 to 1972. He compiled a record that included 880 victories and 4 national basketball championships. Only when he was close to retirement did Rupp open his team to blacks. In the 1966 national finals, a Rupp-led all-white Wildcat team lost to tiny Texas Western, which had five black starters. But the university's one-time reluctance to accept African-American basketball players is a thing of the past. In 1997 an African-American named Tubby Smith became the Wildcats' head coach, and he led Kentucky to a national championship in his first season. ◾

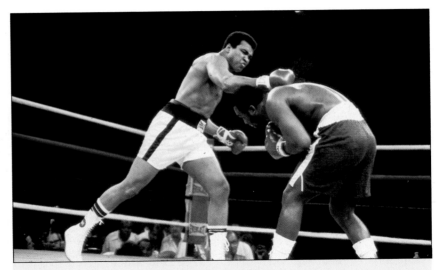

Muhammad Ali

Born Cassius Clay in Louisville in 1942, he was one of the most famous boxers ever. At age twenty-two, he converted to Islam and changed his name to Muhammad Ali. In the ring he was feared for his lightning-quick punches. Outside the ring he made up rhymes to describe his style: "I float like a butterfly, sting like a bee." In the 1960s, Ali stirred controversy when he refused to serve in the army during the Vietnam War. Court cases stemming from his refusal to enter the army kept him from boxing for three years during his prime. ◾

Churchill Downs, Home of the Kentucky Derby

More than a racecourse, Churchill Downs is a palace dedicated to the Sport of Kings. Every year on the first Saturday in May the famous Kentucky Derby is held at this shrine in Louisville. The race covers 2.25 miles (3.6 km) and lasts only about two minutes. Enthusiasts call it "the greatest two minutes in sports." Gardens and floral displays add to the color of Churchill Downs on Derby Day. Visitors to Churchill Downs tour the Kentucky Derby Museum and see exciting films of past Kentucky Derby winners. Even nonracing fans thrill to the color and music of Derby Day ▪

Horse racing is sometimes called the Sport of Kings. Certainly it is royal in the hearts of Kentuckians. Horse races took place on the muddy streets of Lexington in the 1770s. The Kentucky Derby, the nation's oldest continually run horse race, has been held in Louisville every year since 1875. Kentucky's racing tradition has produced many champion horses, but none more glorious than Man O' War. Born near Lexington on March 29, 1917, Man O' War entered twenty-one races and won twenty of them. Interestingly, his one loss was to a horse named Upset. A monument near Lexington marks the grave of this amazing animal, probably the most celebrated horse in racing history.

Man O' War, one of Kentucky's most famous racehorses

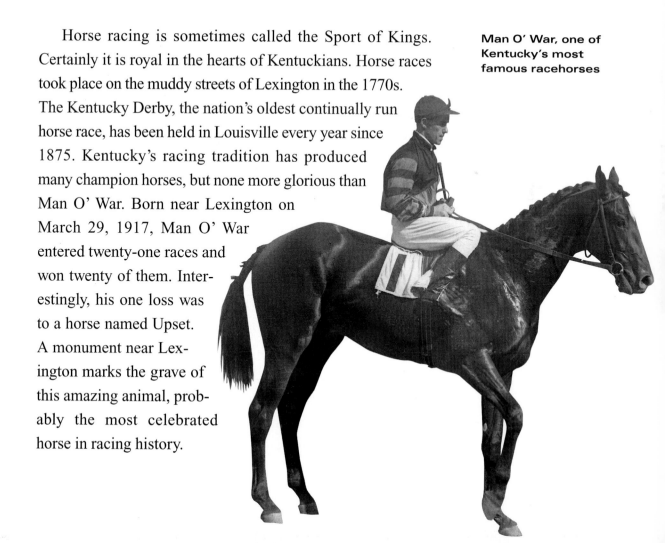

John James Audubon is famous for his drawings of birds.

Arts and Crafts

In the early 1800s, Lexington was hailed as the Athens of the West. Like the Greek city during its Golden Age, Lexington was a gathering place for artists. More portrait painters worked in Lexington than in any other city west of the Appalachians. The most honored portrait painter was Matthew Jouett, who painted leading Kentucky figures including Henry Clay. Many Jouett portraits now hang in Louisville's J. B. Speed Museum. Jouett's neighbor was portrait painter William Edward West. The son of a Lexington inventor and silversmith, West traveled to Europe at a young age. In Europe, West's paintings won the praise of demanding art critics.

John James Audubon was another pioneer Kentucky artist. As a boy, Audubon spent long, lazy days drawing birds. Then he grew up and had to make a living. In 1807, he opened a general store in Louisville. The store failed miserably, and at one point Audubon was jailed for bad debts. He moved to the town of Henderson, Kentucky, where he renewed his boyhood passion of bird drawing. From 1810 through 1819, he painted and roamed the woods of what is now the John James Audubon State Park. His paintings of birds were stunning and dramatic in detail. The Audubon Society, a conservationist group, was later named in his honor. Many of his paintings and his famous book *Birds of America* are now on display at Henderson's John James Audubon Museum.

Henry Faulkner is probably Kentucky's best-known artist of the twentieth century. Born in Simpson County, Faulkner studied in Louisville and later opened a studio in Lexington. Faulkner is famed for his landscape paintings and his renditions of animals.

Another modern figure on the state's art scene is the folk artist Edgar Tolson. Tolson's wood carvings of Biblical figures stand in museums throughout the nation.

In frontier Kentucky the making of craft items was a people's skill rather than the discipline of professional artists. Trying to brighten up their log cabins, the pioneers fashioned baskets, pottery, quilts, furniture, and wooden kitchen utensils. Boys learned how to carve plates and kitchen utensils out of wood. Young woodcarvers also whittled delicate figures of birds and animals to hang on cabin walls. Quilting was a pioneer woman's task, and often one of their most cherished pleasures. Women gathered in groups to

Quilting is among Kentucky's best-known crafts.

sew bright flowers and stars onto quilts. The women chatted and sang songs as they worked.

Creating hand-crafted items is still a Kentucky custom. Especially in eastern Kentucky's mountain communities, people fashion chairs and tables out of native woods. Well-to-do tourists delight in traveling the back roads of eastern Kentucky and stopping at shops to buy handmade furniture.

The Kentucky Highland Museum: Preserving the Crafts

Wonderful hand-crafted items fashioned many years ago by the people of eastern Kentucky are displayed at the Kentucky Highlands Museum in Ashland. The museum is contained in an elegant house built in 1864. A collection of antique handmade clothes valued at more than $400,000 is on permanent display. At the museum, women volunteers demonstrate the art of weaving fabric on looms. Quilting in old Kentucky was an art form. ■

Kentucky Derby Pie

Ingredients:

1/4 lb. (one stick) butter, melted

1 cup sugar

2 eggs, slightly beaten

1 tsp. vanilla

1/2 cup all-purpose flour

2/3 cup chopped pecans

3/4 cup chocolate chips

  9-inch pie crust

Directions:

Preheat oven to 350°F

Mix all ingredients together and pour into the pie crust.

Bake for 40–45 minutes.

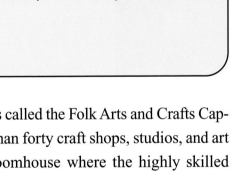

Today, the town of Berea is called the Folk Arts and Crafts Capital of Kentucky. It has more than forty craft shops, studios, and art galleries. Visitors tour the loomhouse where the highly skilled Churchill Weavers turn yarn into baby blankets and sweaters. Special events held in Berea include fairs put on by the Kentucky Guild of Artists and Craftsmen and the Celebration of Traditional Music.

Entertainment in Bluegrass Land

Theater is a Kentucky tradition that dates to frontier times. Some 200 years ago, companies of dancers, musicians, and stunt experts

Early Kentucky Architecture, Palaces of the Pioneers

Log-cabin communities were the norm in pioneer Kentucky. But from the state's beginnings elegant mansions—splendid examples of U.S. architecture—rose from the forests.

One example of an outstand-ing house built during the pioneer era is the mansion at Bardstown called Federal Hill. Construction began on Federal Hill in 1795. It was built out of locally made brick with a stone foundation. The house features a central hall spanned by an elegant arch.

Federal Hill is especially beloved within the state of Kentucky because—legends claim—it inspired Stephen Foster to write "My Old Kentucky Home." ■

A production of *The Wizard of Oz* at the Actor's Theater of Louisville

traveled from village to village to entertain the pioneers. In 1797, a Lexington newspaper, the *Kentucky Gazette,* advertised "an exhibition of tumbling, balancing on a slack wire, and rope walking" to be held at a local tavern.

The state's first permanent theater company opened in Lexington in 1811 under the management of Luke Usher, a professional Shakespearean actor. Usher's family had been friends with Edgar Allan Poe, the writer of macabre stories and poems. Some historians believe Poe's story "The Fall of the House of Usher" was based on Poe's experience with the Usher clan.

Through the years, a love of theater swelled in the Bluegrass State. The Macauley Theater operated in Louisville from 1873 to

The Delights of Kentucky Food

Many Kentucky dishes are unique to the Bluegrass State. Burgoo is a stew that goes back more than 100 years. What's it made of? Who knows! The main ingredient of this special stew can be either chicken or beef. Burgoo recipes vary from family to family and from cook to cook. Usually the stew is spicy and delicious. Fried chicken, country ham, and biscuits with gravy are Kentucky staples. The Hot Brown is a special sandwich (but please don't call it a sandwich) that originated in Louisville's Brown Hotel in the 1920s. An open-faced turkey-on-bread creation, the Hot Brown is now served in many Kentucky restaurants. Enjoy Kentucky's "down home" cooking. ■

1925. Critics lauded the Macauley Theater as one of the best playhouses in the nation. Today, the Actor's Theater of Louisville continues to bring live performances to the city. Summer theater, often performed outdoors, thrives in many towns. Frequently, summer theater plays have themes rooted in Kentucky history. A Bardstown group puts on a musical based on the life of Stephen Foster. The Harrodsburg Pioneer Playhouse presents *The Legend of Daniel Boone*.

Certainly bluegrass music is a highlight of Kentucky's lively entertainment scene. Traditionally, bluegrass music is performed by singers, one or two fiddlers (violinists), a bass player, maybe a mandolin or guitar player, and a banjo player. The groups do not rely on electrical instruments and loud amplification. Songs can be lightning fast, but some are slow and sad to the point where the music provokes tears. Many bluegrass songs tell stories of lost love or echo the lonely voices of people far from home. Always the music has a hypnotic beat that compels finger-snapping or rhythmic clapping.

A Kentucky Fun Fact

Trivia question: What is the most frequently sung song in the United States?
Answer: It's "Happy Birthday to You"; the words and the tune were written by two Louisville sisters in 1893. ■

Musicians at a bluegrass festival

It is said that bluegrass music originated with the settlers who carved farms out of the Appalachian forests. The settlers enjoyed the "mountain string bands" that played at weddings and other festive occasions. This mountain brand of music achieved world fame under William Smith "Bill" Monroe. Born in Rosine, Kentucky, in 1911, Monroe is called the father of bluegrass music. Monroe, who played the mandolin, hosted a popular radio show in the 1940s. It featured his all-Kentucky band—the Blue Grass Boys. From Monroe's group, the ancient mountain string style got a new name— bluegrass. Thus a movement was born and millions of fans around the world today enjoy this special music from Kentucky's soul.

Kentucky is special in many ways. It is special in the love its citizens hold for their home state. That love is visible and ever present in this state. Kentuckians are not ashamed to shed a tear when they sing the chorus of their state song:

Weep no more, my lady,
oh weep no more today.
We will sing one song for the old Kentucky
home,
for the old Kentucky home far away.

Bill Monroe, the father of bluegrass music

Timeline

United States History

The first permanent British settlement is established in North America at Jamestown. **1607**

Pilgrims found Plymouth Colony, the second permanent British settlement. **1620**

America declares its independence from England. **1776**

The Treaty of Paris officially ends the Revolutionary War in America. **1783**

The U.S. Constitution is written. **1787**

The Louisiana Purchase almost doubles the size of the United States. **1803**

U.S and Britain **1812–15** fight the War of 1812.

Kentucky State History

1682 René-Robert Cavelier, Sieur de La Salle, claims the Mississippi basin for France.

1750 Dr. Thomas Walker makes the first thorough exploration of the lands that would become Kentucky.

1767 Daniel Boone first travels to Kentucky

1774 Harrodstown is established as the first permanent white settlement in the region.

1782 Kentucky's last battle of the American Revolution is fought at Blue Licks.

1792 Kentucky becomes the fifteenth state on June 1.

1809 Abraham Lincoln is born on February 12 in a log cabin near the present-day city of Hodgenville.

1848 A slave uprising in Kentucky becomes one of the largest in U.S. history.

United States History

The North and South fight each 1861–65
other in the American Civil War.

The United States is 1917–18
involved in World War I.

The stock market crashes, 1929
plunging the United States
into the Great Depression.

The United States fights in 1941–45
World War II.

The United States becomes a 1945
charter member of the
United Nations.

The United States fights 1951–53
in the Korean War.

The U.S. Congress enacts a series of 1964
groundbreaking civil rights laws.

The United States 1964–73
engages in the Vietnam War.

The United States and other 1991
nations fight the brief Persian
Gulf War against Iraq.

Kentucky State History

1861 The Kentucky state legislature declares its neutrality in the American Civil War.

1862 The Confederate push to take Kentucky is stopped at the Battle of Perryville.

1899 A bitter gubernatorial election ends in a near civil war in the state.

1904–09 The Black Patch War breaks the buying monopoly of large tobacco manufacturers.

1936 The U.S. Treasury establishes a gold vault at Fort Knox.

1948 The University of Kentucky begins accepting black students.

1966 Kentucky's state civil rights laws become the strongest in the nation.

1968 Kentucky becomes the first southern state to pass an open housing law.

1988 The Kentucky Supreme Court rules that the state school system is unconstitutional.

Fast Facts

The capitol

Statehood date	June 1, 1792, the 15th state
Origin of state name	A Wyandot word often translated as "meadowland," "land of tomorrow," or "dark and bloody ground"
State capital	Frankfort
State nickname	Bluegrass State
State motto	"United We Stand, Divided We Fall"
State bird	Kentucky cardinal
State flower	Goldenrod
State fish	Kentucky bass
State gemstone	Freshwater pearl
State song	"My Old Kentucky Home"
State tree	Tulip tree
State wild animal	Gray squirrel
State fossil	Brachiopod
State butterfly	Viceroy
State horse	Thoroughbred

Goldenrod

A Thoroughbred

Kentucky landscape

Black Mountain

State fair	Louisville (mid-August)
Total area; rank	40,411 sq. mi. (104,665 sq km), 37th
Land; rank	39,732 sq. mi. (102,906 sq km), 36th
Water; rank	679 sq. mi. (1,759 sq km), 37th
Inland water; **rank**	679 sq. mi. (1,759 sq km), 32nd
Geographic center	Marion, 3 miles (5 km) northwest of Lebanon
Latitude and longitude	Kentucky is located approximately between 36° 30′ and 39° 9′ N and 82° 00′ and 89° 34′ W
Highest point	Black Mountain, 4,139 feet (1,262 m)
Lowest point	At the Mississippi River, 257 feet (78 m)
Largest city	Louisville
Number of counties	120
Population; rank	3,698,969 (1990 census); 23rd
Density	92 persons per sq. mi. (35 per sq km)
Population distribution	52% urban, 48% rural

Ethnic distribution (does not equal 100%)		
	White	92.04%
	African-American	7.13%
	Hispanic	0.60%
	Asian and Pacific Islanders	0.48%
	Other	0.19%
	Native American	0.16%

Enjoying the Kentucky outdoors

Record high temperature	114°F (46°C) at Greensburg on July 28, 1930
Record low temperature	–34°F (–37°C) at Cynthiana on January 28, 1963
Average July temperature	77°F (25°C)
Average January temperature	34°F (1°C)
Average yearly precipitation	47 inches (119 cm)

Natural Areas and Historic Sites

Mammoth Cave

National Park

Mammoth Cave National Park is the longest recorded cave system in the world.

National Historical Park

Cumberland Gap National Historical Park commemorates the mountain pass in the Appalachian Mountains that was an important route for westward settlers.

National Historic Site

Abraham Lincoln Birthplace National Historic Site contains a replica of the cabin where the sixteenth president of the United States was born.

Daniel Boone National Forest

National Forest

Daniel Boone National Forest covers more than 670,000 acres (271,000 ha).

State Parks

Kentucky supports a wide range of parks and historic site (forty seven in total).

The Cumberland Falls State Resort Park is surrounded by the Daniel Boone National Forest. Situated on the Cumberland River, the highlight of the park is the dramatic Cumberland Falls.

Natural Bridge State Resort Park is also surrounded by the national forest and contains a beautiful, natural stone arch.

The Kentucky Horse Park is popular with tourists and features a great variety of horses and international competitions.

The Jefferson Davis Monument State Historic Site preserves the birthplace of the only president of the Confederacy.

John James Audubon State Park is a bird sanctuary and museum with works by the famous artist.

Old Fort Harrod State Park commemorates the first permanent white settlement in Kentucky.

Fort Boonesborough State Park is the site of the community organized by Daniel Boone.

Blue Licks Battlefield State Park is the site of the bloodiest battle fought in Kentucky during the American Revolution.

My Old Kentucky Home State Park contains Federal Hill, the mansion where Stephen Foster was inspired to write the famous song for which the park is named.

Sports Teams

NCAA Teams (Division 1)

Eastern Kentucky University Colonels

Morehead State University Eagles

Murray State University Racers

University of Kentucky Wildcats

University of Louisville Cardinals

Western Kentucky University Hilltoppers

The University of Louisville

Cultural Institutions

Libraries

Louisville Public Library is the largest public library system in the state.

Transylvania University Library (Lexington) has a notable collection of books on medicine and law.

Filson Club Historical Society (Louisville) has a fine collection on Kentucky history.

Kentucky Historical Society (Frankfort) also contains a large Kentuckiana collection.

Museums

The J. B. Speed Art Museum (Louisville) has a fine collection of European art, Kentucky art, and Native American art.

The Coca-Cola Memorabilia Museum (Elizabethtown)

Kentucky Derby Museum (Louisville)

Allen R. Hite Art Institute at the University of Kentucky (Lexington)

Performing Arts

Kentucky has one major opera company, one major symphony orchestra, one major dance company, and one major professional theater company.

Morehead State University

Kentucky quilt

Universities and Colleges

In the mid-1990s, Kentucky had eight public and twenty-eight private institutions of higher learning.

Annual Events

January–March
Land between the Lakes Eagles Weekend (February)
Humana Festival of New American Plays in Louisville
(March–April)

April–June
Rolex Kentucky 3-day Event in Lexington (April)
Dogwood Trail Celebration in Paducah (April)
Kentucky Derby Festival in Louisville (April–May)
Kentucky Guild of Artists and Craftsmen's Spring Fair
in Berea (May)
International Bar-B-Q Festival in Owensboro (May)
Glasgow Highland Games in Glasgow (June)
Shaker Festival in South Union (late June)

July–September
Kentucky State Fair in Louisville (August)
IBMA Bluegrass Fan Fest in Owensboro
(September)
Corn Island Storytelling Festival in Louisville (September)

October–December
Kentucky Guild of Artists and Craftsmen's Fall Fair in Berea
(October)
Daniel Boone Festival in Barbourville (October)
Allen County Singing Festival (October)
Perryville Battlefield Commemoration (October)
Equifestival of Kentucky in Lexington (October)

North American International Livestock Expo in Louisville (November)
Christmas Sing in the Cave at Mammoth Cave National Park (December)

Famous People

Muhammad Ali

Bud Abbott (1898–1974)	Comedian
Muhammad Ali (1942–)	Boxer
Alben William Barkley (1877–1956)	U.S. vice president
Robert Worth Bingham (1871–1937)	Newspaper publisher
Louis Dembitz Brandeis (1856–1941)	U.S. Supreme Court justice
John Breckinridge (1760–1806)	Politician
Christopher (Kit) Carson (1809–1868)	Trapper and soldier
Albert B. "Happy" Chandler (1898–1991)	Politician and baseball commissioner
Cassius Marcellus Clay (1810–1903)	Politician and abolitionist
Henry Clay (1777–1852)	Statesman
Martha Layne Collins (1936–)	Governor
Jefferson Davis (1808–1889)	President of the Confederate States of America
John Marshall Harlan (1833–1911)	U.S. Supreme Court justice
Abraham Lincoln (1809–1865)	U.S. president
Mary Todd Lincoln (1818–1882)	U.S. first lady
Loretta Lynn (1935–)	Country and western singer

Martha Layne Collins

Bill Monroe

Bill Monroe (1911–1996)	Bluegrass musician
Carry Amelia Moore Nation (1846–1911)	Social reformer
Adlai Ewing Stevenson (1835–1914)	U.S. vice president
Zachary Taylor (1784–1850)	U.S. president
Frederick Moore Vinson (1890–1953)	U.S. Supreme Court chief justice
Robert Penn Warren (1905–1989)	Author
Whitney Moore Young Jr. (1921–1971)	Civil rights leader, educator, author

To Find Out More

History

- Brown, Dottie. *Kentucky*. Minneapolis: Lerner, 1992.

- Fradin, Dennis Brindell. *Kentucky*. Chicago: Childrens Press, 1993.

- Smith, Adam, and Katherine Snow Smith. *A Historical Album of Kentucky*. Brookfield, Conn.: Millbrook, 1995

- Thompson, Kathleen. *Kentucky*. Austin, Tex.: Raintree/Steck-Vaughn, 1996.

Fiction

- Cocquyt, Kathryn, and Sylvia Corbett (illus.). *Little Freddie at the Kentucky Derby*. Gretna, La.: Pelican Publishing Company, 1995.

Holmes, Mary. *Year of the Sevens*. Austin, Tex.: Raintree/Steck-Vaughn, 1991.

Luttrell, Wanda. *Reunion in Kentucky*. Chariot Family Publishers, 1995.

Biographies

- Cavan, Seamus. *Daniel Boone and the Opening of the Ohio River Country*. New York: Chelsea House, 1991.

- Gravelle, Karen. *Growing Up in a Holler in the Mountains: An Appalachian Childhood*. Danbury, Conn.: Franklin Watts, 1997.

- Lawlor, Laurie, and Kathleen Tucker. *Daniel Boone*. Morton Grove, Ill.: Albert Whitman & Co, 1988.

- Marston, Hope Irvin, and Maria Magdalena Brown (illus.). *Isaac Johnson: From Slave to Stonecutter*. New York: Cobblehill, 1995.

- Stone-Peterson, Mary. *Henry Clay, Leader in Congress*. New York: Chelsea House, 1991.

- Wells, Rosemary. *Mary on Horseback: Three Mountain Stories (The Life of Mary Breckenridge)*. New York: Dial Books for Young Readers, 1998.

Websites

- **Commonwealth of Kentucky Homepage**

  http://www.state.ky.us/

  The official home page for the Commonwealth of Kentucky

- **Kentucky Atlas and Gazetter**

  http://www.uky.edu/ KentuckyAtlas/Kentucky-atlas.html

  A comprehensive look at the many highlights of Kentucky

Addresses

- **Kentucky Travel**

  P.O. Box 2011

  Frankfort, KY 40602

  For information about Kentucky travel and tourism

- **Secretary of State**

  State capitol building

  Frankfort, KY 40601

  For information about Kentucky's government

- **Kentucky Historical Society**

  P.O. Box H

  Frankfort, KY 40602

  For information about Kentucky's history

Index

Page numbers in *italics* indicate illustrations.

Meet the Author

I'm R. Conrad Stein. When I was in the Marine Corps in the late 1950s, my best friend was a guy called Sam. Sam grew up on a farm near Bowling Green, Kentucky. In the Marines, he and I served together on Okinawa, thousands of miles from the Bluegrass State. Naturally we talked about home, and when Sam spoke of Kentucky he made the place sound like heaven. I promised to visit him in Kentucky when we both got out of the Marine Corps. I never made the trip, and Sam and I lost contact with each other years ago.

After my discharge from the Marine Corps, I returned to Chicago, where I was born. I attended the University of Illinois and received a degree in history. Later I began to write history and geography books for young readers. Over the years I've published more than eighty books for young people and numerous articles and short stories. I now live with my wife Deborah Kent and our daughter, Janna, in Chicago, and I keep busy writing.

I travel often, for business and for pleasure. Several times I've passed through Kentucky. To prepare for this book I made a special trip to the Bluegrass State. I visited Frankfort, Lexington, Louisville, and drove the back roads, stopping to talk to people wherever I could. Of course, I also read at least a half-dozen books about Kentucky. In Bowling Green I searched the telephone books for any trace of my old buddy Sam. I found nothing. He had told me his family farm was tiny and generated little money. Probably Sam was forced to move elsewhere to make a better living. If someday he sees this book, I hope he remembers me.

Photo Credits

Photographs ©:

Actors Theatre of Louisville: 122 (L. Frank Baum)
AP/Wide World Photos: 9, 50, 55, 56, 84, 115, 134 bottom
Berea College: 113
Corbis-Bettmann: 116, 117, 125, 134 top, 135 (UPI), 38, 52, 66, 76, 118
Dan Dry & Assoc.: 6 top left, 6 top center, 11, 46, 59, 65, 95 top, 96, 99, 106, 107, 109, 111 bottom, 112, 114, 119, 123, 124, 129 center, 130 top, 132, 133 bottom
Dave Bunnell: 69
Dembinsky Photo Assoc.: 91 left, 129 top (Daniel E. Dempster), 91 right (John Gerlach), 63, 77, 131 (Adam Jones), 7 top left, 73 (Skip Moody)
Dixie Gun Works, Union City, Tennessee: 34 top
Envision: 121 (Osentoski & Zoda)
Folio, Inc.: 8, 92 (Everett C. Johnson)
General Motors Corporation: 104
H. Armstrong Roberts, Inc.: 67, 130 bottom (D. Muench), 86, 128 top (W. J. Scott), 82 (D & P Valenti)
James P. Rowan: 79
Jeff Rogers Photography, Inc.: 2, 7 top right, 16, 103 bottom
Kentucky Department of Surface Mining.: 54
Kentucky Department of Travel Development: 120 (Dan Dry), 14, 110
Kentucky Historical Society: 7, 32, 34 bottom, 44
Morehead State University: 75, 133 top

New England Stock Photo: 90 left, 111 top, 128 bottom (Jim Schwabel)
North Wind Picture Archives: 6 top right, 12, 18, 20, 25, 28, 29, 31, 33 bottom, 36, 37, 41 top, 81
Paducah Convention and Visitors Bureau: 83
Patti George: 26, 80
Percy Brown: 61, 129 bottom
Prather & Associates, Inc.: cover
Ric Ergenbright: 72, 87
Stock Montage, Inc.: 17, 21, 22, 24, 33 top, 35, 40, 41 bottom, 42, 43
The Filson Club Historical Society, Louisville, KY.: 47
Tom Till: 7 top center, 19, 64
Tony Stone Images: 62 (Doris De Witt), 98 (Andy Sacks), 58 (Bob Thomason)
Travel Stock: 6 bottom, 90 right, 101 (Buddy Mays)
Unicorn Stock Photos: 71 (Martha McBride);
University of Louisville: 48 (Special Collections Ekstrom Library/Bradley Studio Collection), 49 (Special Collections Ekstrom Library/Caufield & Shook Collection), 51 (Special Collections Ekstrom Library/Lin Caufield Collection)
Viesti Collection, Inc.: back cover, 74 (Bill Terry), 95 bottom, 103 top
Wickliff Mounds Research Center, Murray University: 15
Illustration on page 13 by Jim Railey
Maps by XNR Productions, Inc.